TTIP

For Merel and Larissa

TTIP

The Truth about the Transatlantic Trade and Investment Partnership

Ferdi De Ville and Gabriel Siles-Brügge

polity

First published in 2016 by Polity Press

Polity Press
65 Bridge Street
Cambridge CB2 1UR, UK

Polity Press
350 Main Street
Malden, MA 02148, USA

ISBN-13: 978-1-5095-0101-4
ISBN-13: 978-1-5095-0102-1 (pb)

A catalogue record for this book is available from the British Library.

Library of Congress Cataloging-in-Publication Data

Ville, Ferdi de.
T.T.I.P. : the truth about the transatlantic trade and investment partnership /
Ferdi De Ville, Gabriel Siles-Brügge.
pages cm
Includes bibliographical references and index.
ISBN 978-1-5095-0101-4 (hardback) -- ISBN 978-1-5095-0102-1 (pbk.)
1. European Union countries--Foreign economic relations--United States.
2. United States--Foreign economic relations--European Union countries.
3. North Atlantic Region--Economic integration. I. Siles-Brügge, Gabriel. II. Title.
HF1532.5.U6V55 2015
382'.911821--dc23
2015019452

Typeset in 10 on 16.5pt Utopia Std by
Servis Filmsetting Ltd, Stockport, Cheshire
Printed and bound in the UK by CPI Group (UK) Ltd, Croydon, CR0 4YY

For further information on Polity, visit our website:
politybooks.com

Contents

Abbreviations

ACTA	Anti-Counterfeiting Trade Agreement
AFL-CIO	American Federation of Labour and Congress of Industrial Organizations
ATTAC	Association for the Taxation of Financial Transactions and Aid to Citizens
BEUC	Bureau of European Union Consumer Organisations
BIT	bilateral investment treaty
CEO	Corporate Europe Observatory
CEPR	Centre for Economic Policy Research
CETA	EU-Canada Comprehensive Economic and Trade Agreement
CGE	computable general equilibrium
DG	Directorate-General
ECI	European Citizens' Initiative
EDC	endocrine disrupting chemical
EP	European Parliament

EPA	Environmental Protection Agency
ESF	European Services Forum
ETUC	European Trade Union Confederation
EU	European Union
FDA	Food and Drug Administration
FQD	Fuel Quality Directive
FTA	free trade agreement
GATS	General Agreement on Trade in Services
GATT	General Agreement on Tariffs and Trade
GDP	gross domestic product
GMO	genetically modified organism
HLWG	High Level Working Group on Jobs and Growth
IA	impact assessment
IAB	Impact Assessment Board
INTA	International Trade Committee of the European Parliament
ISDS	investor-to-state dispute settlement
MAI	Multilateral Agreement on Investment
MEP	Member of the European Parliament
MRA	mutual recognition agreement
MRL	maximum residue level
NAFTA	North-American Free Trade Agreement
NATO	North Atlantic Treaty Organisation
NGO	non-governmental organisation
NHS	National Health Service
NTA	New Transatlantic Agenda
NTB	non-tariff barrier
NTM	non-tariff measure
OIRA	Office of Information and Regulatory Affairs

OSHA	Occupational Safety and Health Administration
RCB	regulatory cooperation body
REACH	Regulation on the Registration, Evaluation, Authorisation and Restriction of Chemicals
REFIT	Regulatory Fitness and Performance Programme
RoHS	Restriction of Hazardous Substances Directive
S2B	Seattle-to-Brussels Network
SME	small and medium-sized enterprise
SPS	sanitary and phytosanitary (measures)
TABD	Transatlantic Business Dialogue
TACD	Transatlantic Consumer Dialogue
TAFTA	Transatlantic Free Trade Area
TBT	technical barriers to trade
TNI	Transnational Institute
TPA	Trade Promotion Authority
TPN	Transatlantic Policy Network
TPP	Trans-Pacific Partnership
TRIPS	Agreement on Trade-Related Intellectual Property Rights
TSCA	Toxic Substances Control Act
TTIP	Transatlantic Trade and Investment Partnership
UEAPME	European Association of Craft, Small and Medium-Sized Enterprises
UNECE	United Nations Economic Commission for Europe
US	United States
USTR	United States Trade Representative
WEEE	Directive on Waste Electrical and Electronic Equipment
WTO	World Trade Organisation

Acknowledgements

A lot has happened since we first discussed doing collaborative research on the Transatlantic Trade and Investment Partnership (TTIP), the trade agreement currently being negotiated between the European Union (EU) and the United States (US). We were both attending an academic conference being held in the European Parliament back in April 2013. Much like other 'trade nerds', we were not quite expecting the negotiations to generate as much interest as they have over the past couple of years. Let's face it, trade policy is often seen as an extremely technical, acronym-laden, even soporific area of politics, best left to bureaucrats. While Ferris Bueller has his 'day off' school in the cult 1980s film bearing his name, his history teacher bores the class with a lesson on US tariff policy during the Great Depression (although this in itself is also not an unimportant issue, as we touch upon in the book). At dinner parties and other social gatherings, neither of us was used to talking at much length about what we do in our 'day jobs'. And yet trade policy increasingly has important conse-quences for our 'everyday' lives, not only influencing the price of the goods we consume but, rather, also increasingly shaping the way in which our governments can take action against the health, social and environmental risks we face in our societies. This is why the debate surrounding TTIP – which is all about how trade agreements impact on the ability of governments to regulate in the public interest – is so welcome. Trade is too important just to be left to the experts. The knowledge shown by participants at the many events we have attended over the past two years – from street protests to debates at the European Parliament – gives us hope that the days where trade is seen as 'boring' are numbered.

As a result, we are extremely grateful to the editorial team at Polity for this opportunity to write about TTIP for a broader audience. Our editor, Louise Knight, not only strongly encour-aged us to pursue this project in the first place but has shown a level of interest, dedication and guidance at every stage which we could have only hoped for. We would also like to thank Pascal Porcheron for his excellent editorial assistance, including just the right amount of prodding to ensure we delivered the manuscript in a reasonably timely fashion. While the manuscript's reviewers provided a number of insightful comments that helped greatly in finessing the book's argument, a number of other people took time out of their busy schedules to read parts of the manu-script (or the text in its entirety) and/or offer feedback in other extremely helpful ways. We feel that it is only right that we thank them here: Tony Heron (who also got us thinking about the dis-tinction between 'normative' and 'distributive' trade conflict), Niels Gheyle, Henrik Hermansson, Joelle Dumouchel, Sacha

Dierckx, Nicolette Butler, Dorte Sindbjerg Martinsen, Donna Lee, Jean-Christoph Graz, Jens Ladefoged Mortensen, Yelter Bollen, Marjolein Derous and Stijn Van Wesemael. Any remaining errors are our sole responsibility. Similarly, we would like to thank all those who agreed to be interviewed for this book whom we are unable to name in the interest of preserving their anonymity – and all those individuals who have discussed TTIP with us over the last couple of years and who have immensely enriched our understanding of trade politics. In addition, a big thank you is owed to the University of Manchester Press Office (especially Mike Addelman) and the people at Policy@Manchester (in particular Alex Waddington) for helping us to communicate our research on TTIP to a wider audience.

We wish to thank the publisher Taylor & Francis for allowing us to draw on material (in a significantly revised and expanded form) previously published by us in the following journal article: (2014), 'The Transatlantic Trade and Investment Partnership and the role of computable general equilibrium modelling: an exercise in "managing fictional expectations"', *New Political Economy*, doi: 10.1080/13563467.2014.983059. Gabriel would like to express his thanks to Ghent University's Centre for European Union Studies for hosting him in November–December of 2014. This was an invaluable opportunity to work closely with co-author Ferdi – as well as to put an ear to the ground of the politics surrounding TTIP in Brussels. He is also very grateful to the University of Copenhagen's Department of Political Science for hosting him as a Visiting Scholar (and External Associate on the EuroChallenge research project) over the last few months of book-writing in what has been an extremely stimulating research environment, and to the University of Manchester Politics' Discipline Area for granting him research leave over this period. Finally, Gabriel acknowledges the funding support of the UK Economic and Social Research Council for some of the research featured in this book.

On a more personal note, Ferdi would like to thank his girl-friend Merel – for whom TTIP will not help much in overcoming her lack of interest in trade politics, but who is all the more impor-tant to help remind him that there are so many more significant and enjoyable things than this agreement – and his family, friends and colleagues for all their support and encouragement. Gabriel wishes to thank his long-term partner Larissa for all the support she has given him over the years – particularly in hard times – his friends, especially Chris, Laura and Adrienne, and his family (his father José and his mother Martina, as well as his brother Oscar). This book would not have been possible without all their support.

Ferdi De Ville and Gabriel Siles-Brügge

Ghent and Copenhagen, May 2015

Introduction

Advocates and opponents of the Transatlantic Trade and Investment Partnership (TTIP) agree on very little. But both share the view that the negotiations to create a free trade agreement (FTA) between the two largest economies in the world, the European Union (EU) and the United States (US), represent a 'game-changer'. According to supporters, TTIP is a 'no-brainer', making us all wealthier and allowing the EU and the US to set the standards for the global economy. Critics, on the other hand, warn that TTIP will benefit only big business and leave us all with worse jobs and less environmental, food and health security – undermining our democracy through secretive negotiations and the establishment of corporate tribunals with the right to challenge national laws. George Monbiot has gone as far as to call it a 'full-frontal assault on democracy'. But who is right? What is the truth about TTIP? Will the agreement get us out of the economic crisis and allow Europe and the US to continue exercising global leadership in the twenty-first century, as advocates argue? Or will Europeans soon be buying chicken washed in chlorine and hormone-treated beef without their knowledge and have their democratic policy choices undermined by corporate tribunals, as critics claim?

While the debate has been extremely polarised, we argue that neither of these stark predictions will follow from this agreement.[1] On the one hand, the debate has been centred too much on 'horror stories' and too little on the economic, geopolitical and regulatory effects of TTIP. However, we have also waited in vain for TTIP's proponents to come up with clear, convincing arguments about *how* this deal will lead to the prophesied economic and geopolitical gains they consistently proclaim. Our hope in this book is to move beyond these caricatures of the agreement and try to explore with more rigour what its likely consequences will be.

Although TTIP is far from concluded at the time of writing and its fate remains uncertain, we seek to look at the deal's broader impact on the politics of global trade. These negotiations are already having some interesting unintended consequences (other than filling up the previously relatively bare 'outreach' schedules of academics focusing on trade issues). Even if some of the debate has tended towards oversimplification, it is a generally very welcome development that public interest in trade policy – usually a quite technocratic and secretive policy domain – has increased significantly over the course of the negotiations, with a major mobilisation of civil society groups on the issue. TTIP may not yet have been the subject of a star-studded motion picture like the *Battle in Seattle* – the well-known protests at the 1999 ministerial conference of the World Trade Organisation (WTO). But it is a potential 'game-changer' in its own right and should be seized upon to deepen the debate on twenty-first-century trade policy. This book aims to be a critical contribution to this discussion.

Why TTIP now?

In this book we focus on the motivations for and consequences of TTIP. But, in this section, we first want to set the scene, giving the reader a bit of background on the history of trade relations between the EU and the US and why these negotiations are taking place *now*. Before the TTIP negotiations, the EU and the US discussed trade issues primarily within the multilateral trading system under the auspices of the General Agreement on Tariffs and Trade (GATT), which morphed into the WTO in 1995. At first the US assumed leadership in this system, promoting gradual trade liberalisation in the global economy, with the EU adopting a more proactive leadership position since the Uruguay Round (1986–94). Through a succession of such multilateral trade negotiating rounds since the establishment of the GATT in 1947, tariffs (taxes levied on imports) have been lowered dramatically. Meanwhile, membership of the GATT/WTO expanded significantly, as did the agenda for the negotiations.

In the case of the EU and the US, this new trade agenda has emerged because tariffs have become an almost negligible barrier to imports. Average 'most-favoured-nation' tariffs (those negotiated as a result of the non-discriminatory liberalisation undertaken in the GATT/WTO) are 5.2 per cent for the EU and

3.5 per cent for the US, with both parties actually applying even lower tariffs on each other's imports of under 3 per cent on average (European Commission 2013a: 17). As we will explain in more detail in later chapters, trade negotiators have since the late 1970s increasingly focused on 'non-tariff barriers' to trade (a concept we also unpick later). These include differences in product and services regulation, lack of investor and intellectual property rights protection, closed government procurement markets, and so on. This led to a host of new agreements on such issues during the Uruguay Round. The Doha Round (which kicked off in 2001) was meant to deepen further the reach of the global trading system but has so far failed to deliver on this ambition.

The failure of the multilateral trading system to proceed with 'deep liberalisation' has resulted in first the US and then the EU pursuing economically motivated bilateral FTAs. Both have concluded or are negotiating agreements with a number of mostly (Latin-)American and Asian countries, including Canada, Colombia, Korea, Peru and Singapore, all of which feature 'WTO plus' (that is, going beyond WTO obligations) commitments on trade-related issues. The United States is also at an advanced stage of bi-regional negotiations with eleven Asian-Pacific countries[2] in the so-called Trans-Pacific Partnership (TPP). TTIP thus represents the latest iteration of a broader trend to negotiate an ever-expanding list of 'trade' issues not exclusively within the WTO but through an agreement with a preferred partner.

There are two other factors that are often given as justifications for the start of TTIP negotiations (and which we explore, respectively, in chapters 1 and 2). Firstly, the global financial and economic crisis that started in 2008 is argued to have made external demand a welcome and even necessary source of domestic growth. Secondly, TTIP occurs against the backdrop of the supposed rise of China and other emerging economies vis-à-vis the EU and the US, not only as competitors in global economic *flows* but also as contenders in global economic *governance* – with policymakers across the Atlantic expressing concerns that they are losing geopolitical and global economic relevance. The stagnation of the Doha Round of multilateral trade talks owes much to the rise of these emerging powers, which have broken the EU/US 'duopoly' of global trade governance (Grant 2007; Narlikar 2010).

What is novel about TTIP is the degree of 'deep liberalisation' being sought. Negotiators are explicitly seeking to align EU and US regulatory practices as much as possible. There is, however, also a history to this. The EU and the US tried a number of times after the end of the Cold War to establish a Transatlantic Free Trade Area (TAFTA) and/or Market. The first step in this direction was the 'Transatlantic Declaration' of 1990 in which, for the first time, they institutionalised their bilateral relationship, committing to cooperation on economic, cultural and security issues. But the results soon proved disappointing, due to a lack of interest by Member States and because the Commission was anxious to preserve the EU's own identity before embarking on transatlantic cooperation (Steffenson 2005: 24). Realising that a TAFTA would be too sensitive, in 1995 the EU and the US agreed on the New Transatlantic Agenda (NTA). The main substantive outcomes of the NTA were mutual recognition agreements (MRAs), signed in 1997 for a small number of sectors, intended to eliminate duplicate testing and certification systems. The late 1990s also saw attempts by the EU's Trade Commissioner at the time (Leon Brittan) to establish a 'New Transatlantic Marketplace' that would have substantially removed tariff and non-tariff barriers to trade (Pollack and Shaffer 2001: 16). These plans were ultimately abandoned in 1998 for a much less ambitious and vague 'Transatlantic Economic Partnership', which tried to build the transatlantic market more incrementally. But none of these initiatives really delivered. What is more, on account of administrative resistance on the US side, only two of the six MRAs that had already been signed were ultimately implemented. In the 2000s the EU and the US tried to reinvigorate this process of regulatory cooperation many times, but this has again led to only very limited results. The latest attempt to establish a transatlantic free trade area, before TTIP, was therefore seen as 'over ambitious' and 'unlikely to be realised' (Peterson et al. 2004: 76-9). Overcoming the lack of support for past attempts at transatlantic cooperation may be why policymakers are now so keen to hype up the promise of the current negotiations.

The negotiating process

Having provided a necessarily brief overview of the history of transatlantic trade relations, we now (again very succinctly) introduce the reader to the negotiating process for TTIP and the respective trade policymaking machinery in the EU and the US. The current set of transatlantic trade negotiations trace their origin to a summit in November 2011 between US President Barack Obama, European Council President Herman Van Rompuy and European

Commission President José Manuel Barroso. This set up a High Level Working Group on Jobs and Growth (HLWG), led by the European Commission's Directorate-General (DG) for Trade and the Office of the United States Trade Representative (USTR), which was tasked with identifying how increased trade and investment might contribute to job creation, economic growth and competitiveness. Its final report was published in February 2013 and concluded that 'a comprehensive agreement, which addresses a broad range of bilateral trade and investment issues, including regulatory issues, and contributes to the development of global rules, would provide the most significant mutual benefit of the various options considered' (HLWG 2013: 5).

Following this, the TTIP negotiations were formally announced during President Barack Obama's 2013 State of the Union address. Thereafter, on the EU side, Member States had to authorise the European Commission to start the negotiations (as trade policy is considered to be an EU competence). After some discussion about the negotiating guidelines ('the mandate'), especially on the issue of carving out 'audio-visual services', eventually the Council of the European Union gave the green light in June 2013. Negotiations started one month later. The negotiating teams of both sides – the European Commission and the Office of the USTR, an agency that is part of the Executive Office of the President – meet more or less every two months, alternately in Brussels and Washington, during one-week negotiating rounds (although, so far, one negotiating round has also been held in New York). In between, technical work is done by the negotiating teams in each 'capital'.

The negotiations are divided into three pillars and a larger number of negotiating groups (see Council of the EU 2013). The first pillar of TTIP is 'market access', covering such things as tariff negotiations for goods, services and investment liberalisation, investment protection (including investor-to-state dispute settlement [ISDS]) and government procurement liberalisation. The second pillar refers to 'regulatory cooperation' and is about technical barriers to trade (TBT), sanitary and phytosanitary measures (SPS) or how the EU and the US could cooperate systematically to make present and future regulation[3] more compatible. This is the key pillar of the negotiations and is concerned with bringing about a greater alignment between the EU and the US regulatory systems. The third pillar is dedicated to 'rules' to address shared trade-related issues in areas such as sustainable development, intellectual property rights, energy and raw materials, or trade facilitation.

When (or if?) the negotiations are eventually concluded, the agreement has to be ratified domestically by each party. In the EU, this means that at least a qualified majority[4] of Member States in the Council and a simple majority within the European Parliament have to accept the deal. However, the expectation is that, because of the breadth of the negotiations, making this a 'mixed agreement' with shared competence between the EU and Member States, the deal will also have to be agreed unanimously in the Council and accepted by the parliaments of all twenty-eight Member States (although it can be 'provisionally applied' beforehand; for more on the procedures for EU trade policymaking, see Woolcock 2012: 51–61). On the US side, where Congress is formally given the power to set trade policy under the Constitution, the ratification mechanism depends largely on the preceding decision by Congress to grant the Executive Office 'Trade Promotion Authority' (TPA), also known as 'fast track'. Under TPA, Congress defines negotiating objectives for the USTR and at the end of the negotiations has an 'up-or-down' vote on the agreement without the ability to make amendments. Moreover, under fast track the two chambers have to give their consent to the international agreement with simple majorities, while, without TPA, the Senate needs the higher threshold of a three-fifths majority to withstand a filibuster. A lack of TPA is thus seen as detrimental to the prospects not only of ratifying TTIP but, as a result, also in terms of generating mutual confidence and trust between both parties that TTIP would be given timely and unamended consideration. At the time of writing, Congress had not yet granted the USTR fast-track authority, although there have been important moves in this direction, with the relevant Senate and House of Representatives committees approving their versions of the legislation in April 2015 (Weisman 2015; for more on US trade policymaking procedures, see Destler 2005).

Beyond the hyperbole

The unprecedented level of transparency in the TTIP negotiations shown by EU negotiators (which we discuss in chapter 4) has enormous advantages for us as researchers. We do not have to rely (completely) on leaks and speculation about what is being discussed and decided in the negotiations to be able to participate in a meaningful debate about TTIP while the talks are ongoing. It also allows us to track changes in negotiating positions and seek to explain what has prompted these. That said, a caveat is still in order. To our own frustration as researchers but also to that of several politicians and civil society organisations, not all negotiating documents have been made public (notably, the 'consolidated text' of the agreement remains under wraps). Moreover, as scholars, we should always be wary of strategic considerations when it comes to what is (and what is not) published and when. As a result, this book relies on a number of interviews with EU negotiators and other officials as well as civil society activists and interest group representatives (all of whom were promised anonymity given the contentiousness of the talks). This has allowed us to gain additional insights into actors' motivations and reasoning and to triangulate our interpretations of the negotiations with informed participants. We have further made use of available academic and activist secondary analysis, in the latter case only when it is based on an analysis of appropriate documentation rather than mere speculation.

As critical observers of EU and US trade policy, we analyse the claims that are being made about the consequences of TTIP. But we also keep an eye on claims that are made by the opposition. For example, we do not believe that TTIP will result (directly) in a deregulation bonanza that leads to the acceptance of chlorinated chicken or hormone-treated beef in Europe, but we do think there are a number of underlying concerns that should be taken very seriously.

TTIP is being promoted by two sets of arguments. The first, which we tackle in chapter 1, is that it will bring much desired growth and jobs to the crisis-ridden economies of the US and, especially, the EU. A second narrative, the subject of chapter 2, is that a 'transatlantic market' would be an instrument to preserve the dominant economic position of the EU and the US and contain the geopolitical and geo-economic rise of China and other emerging economies. We dissect these logics and investigate the assumptions on which they are grounded. This leads us to the conclusion that, based on what we already know about the TTIP negotiations, it is very unlikely that these optimistic projections will materialise.

We do not want to end our book here, simply stating what TTIP will not do. Instead, and seeking to do justice to the title, we look for what are likely to be the real consequences and motivations. In chapter 3 we argue that the subtler, but no less important, effects of TTIP (as planned by negotiators) are to bring further discipline to the ability of governments to adopt ambitious market-correcting regulations in the absence of clear scientific proof, imposing strict least-trade restrictiveness and cost–benefit analysis. TTIP is the culmination of a trend towards viewing regulations primarily as irritating barriers to trade, investment and entrepreneurship. The logic and discourse behind it is analogous to domestic attempts to further depoliticise regulatory policies and subject them to an economic logic. The infamous ISDS proposal is only the most obvious example of the way in which this agreement is meant to restrain the primacy of politics in favour of private enterprise.

However, this agenda is running up against considerable headwind from civil society groups, so far principally in Europe. As we illustrate in chapter 4, these have successfully managed to frame the agreement in the public sphere as a threat to democracy and hard-won social environmental and public health protections

– in many ways mirroring the arguments of anti-globalisation protestors at the turn of the century. Opposition is premised on a 'normative' (or value-based) critique of the agreement and its 'deep liberalisation' agenda, far harder for policymakers to suppress with tales of 'growth and jobs and global economic leadership' than previous trade conflicts over distributive questions between various economic interest groups. As a result, we argue that, instead of heralding the depoliticisation of regulatory politics, TTIP has so far led to an increased (re)politicisation of trade policy, usually a technocratic policy domain largely shielded from public scrutiny. In the conclusion, we therefore ask whether and how TTIP may lead to a lasting transformation of twenty-first-century trade politics.

Growth and Jobs

Advocates of TTIP on both sides of the Atlantic are quick to paint the agreement as a massive contribution to 'growth and jobs'. Eliminating remaining barriers to transatlantic trade and investment flows is said to be a boon to businesses, workers and consumers alike. US President Barack Obama has said that TTIP can help support 'millions of good-paying American jobs' (White House 2013a), while UK Prime Minister David Cameron has gone as far as to say that TTIP's economic boost represents a 'once-in-a-generation prize' (cited in BBC News 2013). In the European context these claims have an added significance. With austerity *de rigueur*, TTIP is, in the words of the then EU Trade Commissioner Karel De Gucht, 'the cheapest stimulus package you can imagine' (De Gucht 2013b).

Partly anticipating the controversy that was to engulf the negotiations, EU trade policymakers explicitly recognised this (as well as 'setting global standards'; see chapter 2) as one of the key areas to push in their 'information' (read, *public relations*) campaign surrounding TTIP. In order to support this 'growth and jobs' story, the European Commission contracted a series of econometric studies that intended to show the economic benefits of the agreement. The most significant of these predicted gains for the EU of 0.48 per cent of GDP annually and for the US of 0.39 per cent, and has featured prominently in the discourse of European and US political figures. Given the obvious political importance attached to them, what are we to make of these claims?

In this chapter we interrogate the 'growth and jobs' narrative, focusing in particular on the use of these economic models. We suggest that these serve not only to exaggerate the benefits of TTIP but also deliberately to downplay its potential social costs. As the economic sociologist Jens Beckert (2013a, 2013b) puts it, modelling can be conceived of as an 'exercise in managing fictional expectations'. The uncertainty inherent in modelling social outcomes, which are far more contingent than the calculations of economists, is shrouded from public view. In this vein, the models make unrealistic assumptions about the degree to which TTIP will be able to eliminate barriers to trade (especially given the, at best, mixed record of transatlantic cooperation so far), using biased data gleaned from surveys with business representatives. This, in turn, distracts from the potential costs of the agreement, which are far more difficult to quantify. This includes the social costs of macroeconomic adjustment (as jobs are likely to shift between industries) and the impact of potential deregulation on levels of social, environmental and public health protection. The models and the broader narrative they underpin are an important part of the wider 'politics' surrounding the negotiations, also shaping (as we will illustrate in subsequent chapters) the approach taken by negotiators to seeing regulation in narrow, economistic terms.

A way out of the crisis

In the EU, trade policy has become a central component of its response to the ongoing economic crisis. Facing reduced domestic demand and the realities of austerity, policymakers have argued two things. Firstly, that 'economic recovery will . . . need to be consolidated by stronger links with the new global growth centres' and, secondly, that '[b]oosting trade is one of the few means to bolster economic growth without drawing on severely constrained public finances' (European Commission 2012: 4). Trade policy is being presented as one of the instruments to take Europe out of the crisis. In the words of the Commission again, it '*has never been more important for the European Union's economy*' (European Commission 2013e: 1, emphasis in the original).

EU leaders' public pronouncements on TTIP represent the culmination of this particular rhetoric. De Gucht's statement that the agreement represents 'the cheapest stimulus package you can imagine' is one of the most blatant in this respect, illustrative of a wider tendency to talk of TTIP as a *way out of the crisis*. The US, of course, has not plumped for austerity in the way that the Eurozone has, and therefore the crisis has not taken on as totemic a role in trade policy discourse. That said, the USTR has consistently emphasised the contribution of both TTIP and TPP to 'growth and jobs', a discourse also found at the presidential level in all State of the Union addresses since the start of the TTIP negotiations (White House 2013a, 2014, 2015).

As a result, the EU was not only the *demandeur* of (or party requesting) these negotiations, it has clearly accorded them somewhat more political importance than has the US. It has also largely taken the lead in *selling* TTIP to a potentially sceptical audience. As the Commission acknowledged in a leaked internal memo from November 2013, '[s]trong political communication will be essential to the success of the Transatlantic Trade and Investment Partnership (TTIP), both in terms of achieving EU negotiating objectives and of making sure that the agreement is eventually ratified.' The aim should be 'to define, at this early stage in the negotiations, the terms of the debate by communicating positively about what TTIP is about (i.e. economic gains and global leadership on trade issues)' (European Commission 2013d).

We focus on the latter element of this narrative, 'global leadership', in chapter 2. Our attention here is centred on the idea that TTIP is about 'economic gains' for both parties. In order to bolster this claim, the Commission contracted a series of econometric studies, the most relevant of which was conducted by the London-based think tank the Centre for Economic Policy Research (CEPR 2013). This in turn relies on estimates for non-tariff barriers (NTBs) to trade from an earlier study conducted by the Dutch management consultant firm ECORYS (2009a). The headline figures, quoted time after time by EU officials, but also occasionally by US leaders, are as follows. An 'ambitious' TTIP will generate extra gross domestic product (GDP) for the EU of €119bn annually, or €545 per average household, and €95bn ($120bn) for the US, or €655 ($830) per family.

There have also been a number of other recent modelling exercises of TTIP, which mostly rely on very similar modelling techniques to the CEPR and ECORYS studies (CEPII 2013; ECIPE 2010; Bertelsmann and IFO 2013). In these, TTIP is (in almost all instances) prophesied to have a positive impact on EU and US trade and GDP. But the magnitude of that positive impact varies wildly not only between studies (e.g., between a 0 per cent increase in EU/US GDP in one CEPII scenario and a boost of 4.82 per cent for the US in the Bertelsmann and IFO study) but also within studies. This is because the studies themselves contain various scenarios (as well as a baseline from which the changes in GDP and exports are calculated), from the very modest – eliminating only a small proportion of transatlantic barriers to trade – to the very ambitious – eliminating quite a substantial amount. In public, officials only ever quote the headline figure from the CEPR – which would result from the most 'ambitious' scenario – rather than the *range* of impacts, or the fact that these would materialise only by the year 2027. Moreover, it has been remarked that these headline figures amount only to 'an extra cup of coffee per person per week' (Moody 2014), hardly warranting the bombastic rhetoric used. This brings us to the politics of economic modelling.

Economic modelling and the 'management of fictional expectations'

In what way is economic modelling a political tool? While much has been said about economic discourses in political economy, far less has been said (at least by political scientists) about another powerful form of economic narrative, the ubiquitous use of economic modelling and forecasting. This may be because those working in the field of political economy have sometimes shied away from engaging with quantification and the specific insights of economists (Blyth 2009). This is a real shame, as there is a clear politics behind the use of economic forecasting, which purports to be an exercise in 'objective' and reliable science that is anything but.

Both the EU and the US have a history of (mis)using economic modelling. One of the EU's crowning achievements, the Single Market that eliminated numerous existing NTBs between European economies, is a case in point. Of the most influential Commission papers to come out at the time, the so-called Cecchini report estimated GDP gains from completing the Single Market Programme of between 4.25 and 6.5 per cent (European Commission 1988: 10). This turned out to be wildly exaggerated. Even the Commission's own 2007 Single Market Review estimated the gains to be around half of the lower bound of the Cecchini estimates, at 2.15 per cent (European Commission 2007a: 3). Given such a margin of error in calculating the benefits of the Single Market, what is the value to the EU of the prophesied 0.48 per cent GDP boost from TTIP?

Similarly stark is the use of economic modelling to sell the North American Free Trade Agreement (NAFTA) to a sceptical US audience. While US presidential candidate Ross Perot capitalised on much apprehension about outsourcing and job losses by referring to the 'giant sucking sound' of US jobs being displaced to Mexico, the US government drew on a wealth of econometric studies that all seemed to confirm NAFTA's job-creating and growth-boosting credentials. In some cases the prophesied growth increase was as much as 10.6, 2.1 and 13.1 per cent, for the Canadian, US and Mexican economies respectively (Stanford 2003: 31). These overoptimistic models have since been widely derided, given the finding that there has been 'no visible impact of continental trade liberalization on overall economic growth rates in the three NAFTA member economies' (ibid.: 37). This may explain, at least in part, why US political leaders have been more cautious in their talk about TTIP and less wont to draw on specific figures than their European counterparts. Indeed, in his 2015 State of the Union address, President Obama was 'to admit that past trade deals haven't always lived up to the hype' (White House 2015).

Managing fictional expectations

Our hope here, however, is to go beyond the aphorism attributed to Benjamin Disraeli that there are 'lies, damned lies and statistics' and develop a more sophisticated critique of econometric modelling. In order to do so, we draw on the work of the economic sociologist Jens Beckert (2013a, 2013b) and, more specifically, his idea of 'fictional expectations'. Beckert sees the social world as inherently contingent and the future as fundamentally uncertain. There are far too many intervening factors for us accurately to predict how events will unfold. The extreme example of this is Nassim Taleb's (2007) concept of the 'black swan', an event with dramatic consequences so rare and unpredictable (much like the discovery of hitherto unknown black swans by European explorers in Australia) that its occurrence cannot be inferred from past experience (cue reference to the global financial crisis of 2008). This assumption of fundamental uncertainty distinguishes such work from that of mainstream, neoclassical economists (as well as other rationalist social scientists) who assume that the economy (and society) operates according to well-defined and regular factors that can accurately and reliably be modelled and extended into the future.

If the social and economic future is unknowable, how then do we get by in our social lives? If you are a business owner, how are you able to plan accounts for the year – or order stock on a weekly basis? Beckert argues that we make do with so-called fictional expectations. These are 'imaginaries of future situations that provide orientation in decision-making *despite* the uncertainty inherent in the situation' (Beckert 2013a: 222, emphasis in the original). There is an important analogy here to literary texts in that, in both cases, we are willing to suspend our disbelief, although for very different reasons. In the former this is the entire purpose of a good yarn: what point is there to naysay an unbelievable plotline when this makes for an entertaining story? In the latter, these expectations are essentially a way of muddling through an inherently uncertain social world. In this vein they 'represent future events *as if* they were true, making actors capable of acting purposefully . . . even though this future is indeed unknown, unpredictable, and therefore only *pretended* in the fictional expectations.' Moreover, such expectations are '*necessarily* wrong because the future cannot be foreseen' (ibid.: 226, emphasis in the original).

Of course, not all 'fictional expectations' are the same: a small shop owner ordering groceries on the basis of anticipated sales is not in the same boat as a Wall Street financier speculating on the housing market. While the former's activities would be considered quite normal and routinised – indeed, Beckert sees such practices as necessary to sustain capitalism and markets – the expectations of participants in financial markets are seen as an important determinant of their fragility. Ultimately, as political scientists concerning ourselves with the concept of *power*, we are interested in the idea that '[a]ctors have different interests regarding prevailing expectations and will therefore try to influence them' (Beckert 2013b: 326). This 'management of fictional expectations' is precisely what we would argue is going on in the case of the economic modelling surrounding TTIP.

The politics of economic modelling

Of the economic studies on TTIP, almost all (save the one produced by Bertelsmann and IFO) rely on so-called computable general equilibrium (CGE) models. These models simplify the eminently complex social world out there by reducing it to a number of key variables in order to account for the economic impact of particular policy decisions. For example, they might model the impact that an increase in taxation has on consumption, or (as in this case) whether trade liberalisation leads to increased growth. Within this 'model world' (Watson 2014) individuals are what is called rational utility-maximisers – that is to say, they are always able (and willing) to logically determine their best interests and act upon them. Most importantly, and as the term *general equilibrium* gives away, CGE follows standard economic theory[1] in assuming that the natural state of economic markets is to be in balance. All supply finds its own demand in perfectly efficient and competitive markets (although allowance is sometimes made for non-competitive market structures, as in the CEPR TTIP model). This means that, for every market, all that is produced is consumed and there is no unemployment, as all supply for labour is met with appropriate demand. The whole point of modelling is to assume away the complexity of the economy; the persistence of unemployment, for example, is a clear indicator that all is not well with the world of general equilibrium.[2] All the modeller cares about is generating a simplified equation that captures the relationship in which they are interested (e.g., between taxation and consumption, trade liberalisation and GDP) and which is 'computable', allowing them to plug in data and run a regression that generates concrete figures. In this vein, CGE modelling has grown to become one of the standard forms of modelling the economic impact of policy decisions since it was originally developed in the 1960s (Dixon and Rimmer 2010), especially in the field of trade liberalisation, where the figures used to sell NAFTA were some of the first prominent instances of the use of such models.

In what ways can we speak of a 'management of fictional expectations' when talking about CGE modelling? On the one hand, these are clearly 'fictional expectations' insofar as they produce predictions about the future state of the economy that are intended to guide future action. What is particularly striking, however, is the fact that the forecasts produced are incredibly unreliable. One experienced modeller, Clive George (an architect of trade sustainability impact assessment [IA] in the EU), argues that '[i]n some cases the uncertainty is bigger than the number [generated by such models] itself, such that a number predicted to be positive could easily be negative' (George 2010: 25). The examples we cited above of the Cecchini report and the modelling around NAFTA are cases in point. Beckert's notion that such expectations must by their very nature be wrong because the future cannot be foreseen is thus doubly true, both because of the inherent problem of uncertainty and because the models are unable to generate reasonable forecasts.

But what of the 'management' of these expectations? In what ways can we speak of a deliberate strategy to 'influence' them? We would argue that CGE models do so in at least three ways. First of all, they contain a series of assumptions which are not only unrealistic – undermining their reliability, as highlighted earlier – but which also privilege a particular view of the world (Ackerman 2004). Beyond assuming general equilibrium, the most Pareto efficient[3] and therefore desirable outcome from the perspective of economists, such models appear to be agnostic on other questions, such as the inequalities that may result. As two prominent modellers put it, 'the decisions how to resolve potential trade-offs [between equity and efficiency] must be taken on the basis of societal values and political decisions' (Böhringer and Löschel 2006: 50). However, this agnosticism is anything but. *Values* are a lot fuzzier than numbers, which means they appear far less objective than the 'realities' and 'imperatives' of markets (the domain of the economic modeller). As Fioramonti (2014: 9) puts it, '[m]arkets are more malleable to measurement' than 'social relations and the natural world'. The land value of a national park may be relatively easy to determine, as may tourist revenues associated with it, but it is far harder to quantify what many may call its 'intrinsic value' as a nature reserve (ibid.: 104–43).

More blatant than this broad, implicit bias in CGE models is the power the researcher has to shape the results of their modelling. Just changing the data used, the variables computed or the values on the coefficients in the regression equation can have a massive effect on the results. As even *The Economist* (2006, cited in Scrieciu 2007: 681), a newspaper known for its advocacy of the free market, put it in the case of studies examining the relationship between trade, productivity and growth: '[i]f the [CGE] modeller believes that trade raises productivity and growth ... then the model's results will mechanically confirm this.'

Although they have come under increasing fire from economists, CGE models are powerful political tools for a third reason. They are essentially 'black boxes' (Piermantini and Teh 2005: 10), often impenetrable to most lay readers unfamiliar with general equilibrium theory. This serves to shield their biases and lack of reliability from public view. We are willing to 'suspend our disbelief' because we simply have no means of doing otherwise. It is no wonder that the heterodox economist Ha-Joong Chang (2014) has called on the public to become more economically literate! In this spirit, it is time to look at how CGE modelling has been used to shield TTIP from criticism, starting with the exaggerated benefits of the agreement. Before we turn to this, however, it is important to stress that we are not seeking to engage in a detailed, technical critique of the econometric modelling used for TTIP or to generate our own figures. Rather, what we are doing is pointing to the inherently *political* nature of modelling.

Modelling TTIP

How have the modellers come up with TTIP 'growth and jobs' figures? Here we focus specifically on the CEPR model, as this has had the greatest prominence. It was not only announced with some fanfare by a Commission press release in March 2013 (European Commission 2013f) but was also the basis for the EU's own 'Impact Assessment' of TTIP (European Commission 2013a). These are also the figures that are most likely to be quoted by advocates of TTIP. But, while many of the assumptions we drill into here are specific to the CEPR (2013) model, the broader arguments are more widely applicable. Most of the studies of TTIP's economic impact use CGE modelling. They therefore make very similar simplifying assumptions, use very similar trade data, and are open to very similar biases as the CEPR report.

First, we must examine what sort of assumptions the modellers have built into their study. The model features a number of different scenarios – or assumed outcomes from EU–US negotiations – for which different results are generated. The first of these is a so-called baseline scenario, which assumes that no trade deal is signed. All the other scenarios are assessed against this benchmark and include ones that assess the effect of only removing tariffs or only eliminating barriers to trade in services or to government procurement (the purchasing of goods and services by public bodies). The variety of scenarios in this (and indeed other models) explains the large variation in the results we noted earlier.

At the upper end of the CEPR estimates is the most important scenario – the only one habitually quoted by supporters of the agreement. This assumes that a 'comprehensive' and 'ambitious' FTA will be signed between the EU and the US, covering all manner of barriers to trade. More specifically, it assumes that TTIP will eliminate all tariffs on goods traded between the EU and the US and remove 25 per cent of all NTBs restricting trade in goods and services. This 25 per cent figure includes eliminating 50 per cent of barriers in the field of government procurement. The study also makes an allowance for 'spillover effects'; both exporters in the EU/US and those in third countries might benefit from fewer transatlantic barriers to trade and from TTIP's assumed effect in terms of leading the rest of the world to align its standards with the new 'transatlantic marketplace'. Making these assumptions leads the modellers to the following (in)famous results: extra GDP per annum of 0.48 per cent in the case of the EU and 0.39 per cent in the case of the US, or €119 billion for the EU and €95 billion for the US (CEPR 2013: 2).

Are these assumptions reasonable? Will TTIP deliver all that is being promised? As figure 1.1 clearly illustrates, a vast majority of the estimated gains for both the EU and the US ultimately comes from the hypothesised reductions in NTBs and *not* from tariff elimination. In the case of the EU, a whole 59 per cent of the GDP gains come from regulatory alignment (and only 23 per cent from eliminating tariffs), while for the US this figure is a whopping 74 per cent (with only 11 per cent of the gains coming from eliminating tariffs)! How hard could it possibly be to eliminate 25 per cent of existing regulatory barriers to trade? Surely a quarter of these is not that much to ask negotiators to tackle?

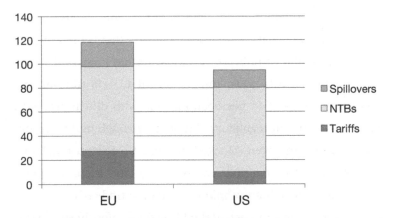

Figure 1.1 Breaking down the gains from trade liberalisation in TTIP,
€ billions

Source: *Adapted from De Ville and Siles-Brügge (2014b: 13).*

Overblowing the benefits

Our argument is that this is a far more heroic assumption than
the modellers are implying. For one, only 50 per cent of NTBs
between the EU and the US are even considered 'actionable'
within the data used by the study. In other words, only half are
the direct result of policy decisions that can be addressed through
a trade agreement such as TTIP (CEPR 2013: 27). Other NTBs
include such things as consumer tastes, which are beyond the
scope of a trade agreement. Thus, for example, TTIP could theoretically remove regulatory barriers to the selling of genetically
modified organisms (GMOs) in Europe, but it could not possibly
directly shape European consumers' oft-remarked suspicion of
such products. So 25 per cent of all NTBs turns into 50 per cent
of 'actionable' NTBs, an altogether more significant proposition.

Moreover, the definition of what is 'actionable' is also pretty *generous*, insofar as it includes any measure that is theoretically within the realm of policy to address. As we suggested in the introduction to this book, the history of EU–US transatlantic regulatory cooperation has been plagued with difficulties; even modest attempts at regulatory alignment through mutual recognition agreements were blocked because US federal regulators were keen to preserve their ability to regulate. There have also been a number of high-profile transatlantic trade disputes over differences in the approach of the EU to food safety in such areas as hormone-treated beef or GMOs (Pollack and Shaffer 2009).

The prospects for bridging such differences are relatively slim, especially if we consider the two main sectors expected to gain from the agreement. These are automobiles and chemicals, together accounting for 59 per cent of the expected increase in exports for the EU from TTIP (and 54 per cent in the case of the US; authors' calculation based on data from CEPR 2013: 64, 66). In the case of chemicals, much has been made of the EU's 'precautionary approach' to regulation under the Regulation on the Registration, Evaluation, Authorisation and Restriction of Chemicals (REACH) – where the burden of proof lies on manufacturers to show that their chemicals are safe before they are authorised – and the US's laxer 'science-based' approach, which puts the burden on the Environmental Protection Agency (EPA) to show that chemicals are noxious (Vogel 2012: 154–78). The EU and the US are so far apart on this issue that the Commission itself has been forced to admit at the start of the negotiations that 'neither full harmonisation [the creation of a common EU/US standard] nor mutual recognition [where both sides accept each other's standards] seems feasible on the basis of the existing framework legislations in the US and EU: [these] are too different with regard to some fundamental principles' (European Commission 2013g: 9).

But what about automobiles? These are the poster child of advocates of TTIP insofar as it is generally acknowledged that car and other motor vehicle safety standards are broadly compatible across the Atlantic (ECORYS 2009a: 44, 46–7). Few would quibble about the exact positioning of headlamps, the colour of indicator lights, or some of the more technical specifications for seat belts. But, while regulatory outcomes might not differ greatly in this sector, regulatory alignment faces the prospect of multiple jurisdictions in the US (due to variations in state emissions policies) – as well as important differences in the way in which conformity with such standards is assessed. As the Commission was also forced to admit in its position paper for the negotiations, mutual recognition of technical requirements 'could not be extended to conformity assessment, in view of the wide divergence between conformity assessment systems (prior type approval in the EU, in accordance with the United Nations Economic Commission for Europe [UNECE] system, and self-certification with market surveillance in the US)' (European Commission 2014c: 2, emphasis added). Moreover, the view that regulatory convergence for the automobile sector is somehow 'easy' to achieve – what often gets referred to as the 'low-hanging fruit' of the negotiations (Lester and Barbee 2014) – ignores the zeal with which the powerful, independent US regulators have clung on to their independence, as the past experience of the EU–US regulatory cooperation in the 1990s shows, where the Food and Drug Administration (FDA) and the Occupational Safety and Health Administration (OSHA) blocked the implementation of a series of MRAs (House of Lords 2013: 3–4).

Even if an agreement brings a breakthrough in one or the other sector, the gains from TTIP are hardly assured, as the modelling assumes important interlinkages between sectors. In other words, it assumes regulatory alignment *across all sectors*; in an interconnected economy based on various supply chains, the effects of dealing with regulatory barriers in one sector clearly cut across others. For example, reducing barriers for chemical producers will have an important knock-on effect for industrial users of chemicals as well as any of their other business customers or end users. Thus, figures taken from the ECORYS 2009 study – which provides the figures on NTBs for the EU and the US for the CEPR study – show that adding up liberalisation in each sector produces only roughly a quarter of the gains for the EU and a third for the US when compared to liberalisation *across the board* (ECORYS 2009a: xxi–xxii). If we liken TTIP to an attempt at toppling a chain of dominoes, taking out any one tile (or sector) is likely to affect the end result drastically.

To top it all, there is also evidence of bias in the NTB figures themselves, which were produced with the help of a number of EU and US business representatives with a strong interest in the conclusion of negotiations (see chapter 3). They derive from a combination of discussions with forty sectoral experts with close ties to business, literature reviews – carried out by these sectoral experts 'supported by' ECORYS and a number of transatlantic business groups – as well as a 'business survey' with around 5,500 participants (ECORYS 2009a: 9–10). As the authors of one critical study have noted, such business actors (and those close to them) have a clear interest in exaggerating both the cost of NTBs and the degree to which TTIP might be able to address them (in the jargon, their 'actionability') (Raza et al. 2014). On the first point, the literature review, business survey and sectoral experts esti-mated that NTBs added, respectively, around 10, 7 and 8 per cent to transatlantic trade costs (ECORYS 2009a: 9), when other stud-ies have suggested a much lower figure, in the region of 3 per cent (Raza et al. 2014: viii).[4] On the issue of whether these NTBs can be addressed through policy, the verdict is similar: the business representatives and others consulted in preparing the data may well 'exhibit a tendency to overestimate actionability. Thus, the determination of actionability is basically a more or less sophisti-cated guess of a group of persons with vested interests' in talking up the potential of TTIP (ibid.: 21).

It is important to stress at this point that we are also trying to avoid falling into the same trap of making steadfast predictions as the econometric studies. Even if TTIP leads to significant liber-alisation, predicting this at the start with problematic models is a clear example of managing fictional expectations (which are '*nec-essarily* wrong' because the future cannot be foretold), especially so given the past history of limited integration, the limitations to liberalisation in TTIP acknowledged by the Commission itself, and the clear bias in the NTB figures.

Downplaying the potential costs

The 'management of fictional expectations', however, goes beyond the specific assumptions of the studies or their use of problematic data. Rather, talking of the 'huge' (and costless) boost given to EU and US growth and jobs allows policymakers to talk down some of the potential costs of the agreement. It privileges what *can* (in a very flawed way) be measured – future economic gains – over what is more difficult to quantify – the broader social and/or environmental impact of the agreement. As is argued in what follows, these include the broader economic costs of adjusting to freer trade and the potential deregulation that might come from aligning standards. This is the great fear expressed by opponents to the deal (see chapter 4).

'Macroeconomic adjustment costs' (to use their more technical name) may include such things as losses in tariff revenue, destabilising changes in the trade balance, and the 'displacement' of workers from uncompetitive industries (Raza et al. 2014: v–vi). Of course, statistics can be mustered to account for such developments: the CEPR study itself comes up with an estimate of between 400,000 and 1.1 million jobs being 'displaced' (workers being shifted from one job to another; ibid.: iv). But the assumption, following *general equilibrium* theory, is that this is a mere 'displacement' of workers from one sector to another; to rephrase a much derided line often (erroneously) attributed to the then British Conservative cabinet minister Norman Tebbit, workers will simply 'get on their bikes' and find new work. Overall, there will be no increase in unemployment. This downplays not only the unequal distribution of gains from TTIP – as with any trade agreement, a number of sectors in both the EU and the US stand to lose from an agreement liberalising trade – but also the wider social costs of unemployment. The assumption is that the economy will be able unproblematically to adjust to external competitive pressures, which is not entirely consistent with the experience of several deindustrialised regions in Europe and the US (Northern England and the 'Rustbelt' spring to mind). This point has not been lost on high-profile critics of TTIP and TPP in the US (such as Joseph Stiglitz, Robert Reich, Clyde Prestowitz or Paul Krugman) in the context of ongoing debate on renewing 'fast-track' negotiating authority (Krugman 2014; Stiglitz 2014; Reich 2015; Prestowitz 2015).

Even more significant, given TTIP's focus on regulation, is the potential deregulatory impact the agreement may have. While we discuss this in more depth in chapter 3, here it is important to underscore how the modelling deliberately downplays the impact of such a development. As noted by other critics, 'the elimination of NT[B]s will result in a potential welfare loss to society, in so far as this elimination threatens public policy goals (e.g. consumer safety, public health, environmental safety)' (Raza et al. 2014: vi). It is thus somewhat disingenuous for the modellers to argue that their studies do 'not judge whether a specific NT[B] is right or wrong or whether one system of regulation is better than the other'. Focusing on the objective of 'identifying divergences in regulatory systems that cause additional costs or limit market access for foreign firms' (ECORYS 2009a: xxxv) can hardly be called a neutral exercise. It paints these 'divergences' as mere 'barriers' to trade to be removed – rather than potentially serving a legitimate social purpose (on how the benefits of regulation are downplayed; see Myant and O'Brien 2015). Moreover, the future deregulatory impact of TTIP is not only very difficult to measure but also *fundamentally uncertain*, which makes it difficult to counter the 'hard' figures of the modeller (which are of course anything but objective).

In this vein, both the modellers and the European Commission have sought to downplay the uncertainty underpinning the CEPR study. Instead, this is presented as eminently reasonable and even cautious in its conclusions. The modellers characterise their assumptions regarding the degree of NTB liberalisation as 'relatively modest', while also emphasising the advanced nature of their CGE modelling (CEPR 2013: 21–2, 27). The Commission, for its part, has stated that this study uses a 'state of the art' model with assumptions 'as reasonable as possible to make it as close to the real world as possible'. The model, moreover, also lies 'at the mid-range of most other studies carried out on TTIP', with '[t]he Commission believ[ing] in a conservative approach to analysis of policy changes' (European Commission 2013h: 2–3). No 'health warnings' are attached, as doing so might undermine the model's usefulness as an exercise in 'managing fictional expectations'.

Contesting economic modelling

Numbers have become a key battleground in the fight over TTIP. Seeking to shape the debate on the agreement 'on its own terms', the Commission sponsored a study that seemed to show 'significant' economic gains from 'cutting red tape' across the Atlantic – up to €545 per family of four in the EU (or $830 for a family in the US). Since its publication, however, there has been growing scepticism, especially as the methodology is increasingly said to be 'based on unrealistic and flawed assumptions' (Raza et al. 2014: vii). A 2014 European Court of Auditors report on the Commission's management of preferential trade agreements found that it had 'not appropriately assessed all the[ir] economic effects'. It also included an entire annex on the 'Limitations of the CGE model' the Commission had been so wont to use in its assessments of trade agreements (European Court of Auditors 2014: 8, 45). The irony behind all of this is of course that a CGE model is being used to justify a trade agreement that is supposed to lift the EU out of the crisis, when a permutation of such general equilibrium models (more specifically, dynamic stochastic general equilibrium modelling) completely failed to predict the advent of the 2007–8 Financial Crisis (Watson 2014).

What is even more interesting from our perspective is that the *presentation* of this modelling by the Commission has been widely criticised by civil society groups. In a letter from non-governmental organisations (NGOs), the Commission has been accused of 'exaggeration' (for citing only the upper econometric estimates), providing insufficient information on 'time scale' (for not citing that the gains will materialise only by 2027) and of 'us[ing] obfuscating language . . . that is very difficult to understand for lay persons' (BEUC and Friends of the Earth Europe 2014: 1–2) – all features of the management of fictional expectations we described above. The danger is that, having caught on to this, some have sought to fight fire with fire, seeking to quantify the negative impact of the agreement. One study – prominently invoked by critical actors and making use of an alternative, Keynesian methodology that does not assume full employment (the UN Global Policy Model) – speaks of 600,000 lost jobs across the EU and GDP losses of 0.07, 0.29 and 0.48 per cent in the UK, Germany and France respectively (Capaldo 2014). There are also attempts (ongoing at the time of writing) to measure the deregulatory impact of TTIP.[5] But, much as the gains from TTIP are impossible to predict, we must be intellectually honest and accept that its potential costs are 'subject to considerable uncertainty', especially while the talks are still taking place (Raza et al. 2014: iv). Even once the negotiations on TTIP are concluded, we would contest the notion that you can simply reduce the impact of the agreement on social, environmental and public health regulation to a series of economic statistics. This is falling into the trap of accepting the broader normative biases of econometric modelling.

Moreover, while there may be increased contestation of the numbers behind TTIP that feeds into a critical narrative about the negotiations (see chapter 4), advocates have fought back. While they have toned down the rhetoric to speak about 'growth and jobs' more generally (without necessarily invoking specific figures), there has also been a push to emphasise the benefits of TTIP in terms of 'cutting red tape'. This is said to benefit not just large, multinational exporters but also small and medium-sized enterprises (SMEs). In the words of the USTR Michael Froman (2015), '[m]any people assume exporting is a game that's limited to big businesses, but in reality, 98% of our 300,000 exporters are small businesses.' Both he and his counterpart, the European Trade Commissioner, have been keen to emphasise the potential of TTIP for such small businesses, frequently citing examples of specific SMEs that would benefit from a freer transatlantic marketplace (Froman 2014; Malmström 2015a).[6] Meanwhile various business organisations have produced reports based on case studies of various SMEs that are said to gain from a reduced transatlantic regulatory burden (e.g., British American Business 2015).

It is thus clear that numbers and claims of economic gains remain a key arena in the battle for TTIP. Another is the argument that the agreement will allow the EU and the US to shape the face of global economic governance for years to come. We discuss this next.

2

Setting Global Standards

Besides being the 'silver bullet' bringing much needed growth and jobs to the EU and the US, a second argument for TTIP is that it will allow both parties to continue setting the standards for the global economy in the twenty-first century. Arguments of a strategic, geo-economic and geopolitical nature have been increasingly prevalent, accompanying the more traditional economic case for FTAs of enhanced efficiency, increased income and additional employment.[1] This 'setting global standards' discourse serves a double function. By emphasising the prospect that China and other emerging economies might in the near future be masters of global economic governance if the EU and the US fail to cooperate, (progressive) sceptics of TTIP are being accused of contributing to the West's demise. At the same time, by invoking the idea of China as 'the other', the impression is strengthened that the regulatory cultures of the EU and the US are rather similar, paving the way for regulatory cooperation. This chapter critically examines the assumptions and consequences of this narrative.

Even before the financial crisis erupted in 2008, which seemingly harmed developed economies more than emerging economies, there had been a lot of talk about the (economic) 'decline of the West and the rise of the rest' (Zakaria 2009). In particular, the BRIC countries (Brazil, Russia, India and China) – a term coined in 2001 by Jim O'Neill, then of Goldman Sachs – have been seen as posing a challenge to the postwar dominance of the US and (later also) the EU over the global economy. Since then, there has been an increasing awareness in American and, especially, European policy circles of their declining hold over global economic governance. This view has been reinforced by the failure to conclude the Doha Round in the face of resistance from India and (to a lesser extent) China. All of this has led key political actors on both sides of the Atlantic, such as Secretary of State Hillary Clinton or the then North Atlantic Treaty Organisation (NATO) Secretary-General Anders Fogh Rasmussen, to refer to TTIP as an 'economic NATO' (van Ham 2013: 2; Rasmussen 2013).

The logic behind this argument runs as follows. Only by sticking together can the EU and the US counter their slide into economic and geopolitical irrelevance. A 'Transatlantic Common Economic Space', as Barroso (2014) referred to it, with common norms and rules that would cover nearly half of the world's GDP and one-third of the world's trade, would enable Europeans and Americans to continue setting the rules of globalisation. It is 'now or never', because, in only a couple of years' time, China will be the largest economy in the world and the global rule-setter, with the once powerful Western governments relegated to becoming rule-takers. This narrative has only emerged as more central to advocacy in favour of TTIP as the world, and Europe in particular, has seemingly become a more insecure place, with turmoil both at the EU's southern border with the Arab world and in its eastern neighbourhood, given conflict with Russia over Ukraine. In this turbulent geo-economic and geopolitical environment, advocates of transatlantic economic integration point to the relative homogeneity of European and American interests and values, which should not be disrupted by the relatively small differences of opinion of the past (or those emerging now in the context of the TTIP negotiations).

This second key narrative of 'setting global standards' in the face of the rise of the likes of China thus provides an additional argument to convince those who are rather sceptical about the 'economic gains' narrative discussed in the previous chapter. The more the economic rationale, and TTIP in general, has been contested, the more this second, geo-economic justification has been drawn upon. It is a forceful one, particularly because there is a thinly veiled threat directed at those who fear that TTIP would negatively affect the quality of social, environmental or public health regulation (especially in the EU), arguably the key concern of critics (see chapter 4). The alternative to cooperating across the Atlantic now, proponents warn, is that standards will be decided within a couple of years by China, which is far less concerned about such matters as social and environmental protections. 'Is that what you want?' seems to be the subtext.

This narrative appears to hold some sway among key policymakers. In the EU, many Social Democrats, who have mixed feelings about TTIP, are crucial to securing a majority in the

European Parliament in favour of the agreement and are also in government in a number of important Member States, such as France, Italy and Germany. In Germany, there has been an intense debate about TTIP, especially with regard to food safety and ISDS (see chapters 3 and 4). But, in February 2015, the German Social Democratic Economy Minister Sigmar Gabriel spoke out strongly in favour of TTIP – revising a more hesitant position taken earlier on – saying that failure to agree an ambitious deal would cost the EU influence in the global economy (Fox 2015). Responding to opponents of Trade Promotion Authority within his own Democratic Party, President Obama has also increasingly invoked this argument.

In the remainder of this chapter, we scrutinise this geo-economic narrative. We briefly review debates on the US and EU position in the post-Cold War global political economy. These discussions have gone from speaking of US-dominated unipolarity, to an EU soft power-based challenge of US hegemony, to, most recently, the notion that both Western powers are in decline with respect to emerging markets. It is this latter perception that has led to the conclusion that the EU and the US need to join hands in shaping global economic governance. Being able to set the global rules here is a particularly important objective for the EU, which, in the absence of developed military capacity, considers its 'market power' to be its main source of strength in global politics. We warn, however, that EU–US regulatory cooperation will not automatically result in the setting of global standards, as TTIP's champions claim.

Notably, we draw an important distinction between the consequence of *harmonisation* and the *mutual recognition* of regulations when it comes to the standard-setting capabilities of TTIP. The latter not only carries the risk of setting off a 'race-to-the-bottom' dynamic in terms of the levels of risk regulation across the Atlantic but will also provide little or no incentive for third countries to align their norms and rules with those in the EU and the US. There is also a second problem with the 'setting global standards' argument in favour of TTIP. Key to the narrative of transatlantic regulatory leadership is emphasising similarity in the regulatory objectives and philosophies on both sides of the Atlantic, in contrast to the view in the first decade of the twenty-first century that the EU and US regulatory philosophies fundamentally conflict with each other. Belittling the distinctiveness of the EU's approach to market regulation might decrease rather than promote, we caution, the prospect of ambitious global standards in the future.

American decline and disillusion with market power Europe

The view that the US and the EU currently need to collaborate to prevent China from becoming the next regulatory superpower is presented as common sense. In the US, this resonates with the idea of American hegemonic decline in the global economic and political system that has been around through several waves of 'declinism' (Huntington 1989). While in the early Cold War era the fear was that the US was losing strength relative to the Soviet Union, Japan emerged as the main commercial bogeyman in the 1970s and 1980s – with concern over the relative competitiveness of the US compounded by persistent trade deficits. In contrast, the period after the end of the Cold War, and certainly after the Japanese asset price bubble of the 1990s and its subsequent (long) lost decade, has been defined as the American unipolar era – a moment when its model of liberal capitalism triumphed over alternatives. The dominant view, however, is far less sanguine these days, with the 'Chinese threat' being taken more seriously than previous challenges to US power: 'this time is (allegedly) different' to previous episodes of relative decline, among other things because the US's traditional allies are also losing (economic) clout at around the same time (Rachman 2012).

European integration has always been pursued (at least partly) with an eye to achieving equivalence in economic and political power with the US. And for a decade or so, from the mid-1990s to the mid-2000s, EU policymakers and some observers – looking beyond military capabilities – seemed to agree that the EU's 'soft power' would allow it to lead in the twenty-first century. This was in part *because of* the distinctiveness of its geopolitical and socioeconomic policies from those of the US. But the protracted effects of the economic crisis have shattered hopes of a European century based on such normative leadership.

In what follows, we unpick the narrative that presents transatlantic cooperation as a matter of course to counter Western decline. We show how, during the brief period where there was optimism about the EU's regulatory or market power, it was seen as a counterweight to the US rather than as a likeminded partner, as in the discourse surrounding TTIP. We then challenge the idea that transatlantic regulatory cooperation would automatically translate into continued EU–US global leadership.

Shared values?

How things change. While today EU and US leaders emphasise the importance of partnership, only a decade ago the transatlantic relationship was strained over disagreements about the war in Iraq and how to deal with terrorist threats more generally, as well as about the urgency of and the way to fight climate change or the right approach to protect citizens against uncertain environmental and food safety risks through the application of the 'precautionary principle' (the notion that regulators should adopt measures even in the absence of unambiguous scientific evidence of risk). The EU and the US were engaged in fierce disputes before the WTO Dispute Settlement Body on the EU's ban on hormone-treated beef, chlorinated chicken and a *de facto* ban on GMOs. In the same period, the US State Department lobbied heavily against the EU's new (and very strict) system for the regulation of chemicals (REACH), as well as against similar strict regulations on recycling obligations for electrical and electronic equipment (the Directive on Waste Electrical and Electronic Equipment [WEEE]) and bans on hazardous substances in electrical and electronic equipment (the Restriction of Hazardous Substances Directive [RoHS]). In addition to the Kyoto Protocol on climate change, the US had failed to ratify a number of international environmental agreements championed by the EU, such as the Stockholm Convention on Persistent Organic Pollutants, the Basel Convention on Hazardous Waste, the Rotterdam Convention on Hazardous Chemicals and Pesticides, and six of the eight core labour conventions of the International Labour Organisation. Reflecting on such developments, Robert Kagan famously opened his book *Of Paradise and Power* (2004: 3) with the words '[i]t is time to stop pretending that Europeans and Americans share a common view of the world, or even that they occupy the same world.' This divergence between the EU and the US coincided with a period of self-assurance on the European side about its ability to influence the world through lofty norms and rules.

After the perceived success of the new 'euro' currency and the 'big bang' Eastern European enlargement of 2004, and not-withstanding the rejection by the French and Dutch electorates of the Constitutional Treaty, there was much confidence about the European integration project (Cafruny and Ryner 2007). It is indeed difficult to imagine today, after just over five years of economic, political and social crisis in the EU (and the euro area in particular), that the first decade of the twenty-first century was marked by considerable enthusiasm about the power and prospects of the EU – if not amid the general public then at least among a number of important policymakers and political pundits. One of the most talked-of books in international politics of the period was Mark Leonard's *Why Europe Will Run the 21st Century* (2005), which spoke of the EU's ability to influence the rest of the world through its soft, regulatory power. The year after, the then Belgian Prime Minister Guy Verhofstadt published *The United States of Europe* (2006), pleading for a more deeply integrated EU that could leave its mark in a globalised world. The American Ambassador to the EU at the time, Rockwell Schnabel, declared wistfully, '[l]et's face it – you have to deal with them. They have the power of that Market' (Fuller 2002). Even *The Economist* (2007), not always known for its Euro-enthusiasm, featured the following headline in 2007: 'Brussels rules OK: how the European Union is becoming the world's chief regulator'. In this vein, the investigative journalist Mark Shapiro's book *Exposed: The Toxic Chemistry of Everyday Products and What's at Stake for American Power* (2007) argued that the US was failing to protect its citizens from dangerous substances and products in the way the EU was doing and was therefore rapidly losing its (soft) power to shape the world.

Academics have touted the EU's regulatory power for even longer. As far back as 1995, David Vogel argued that the EU, thanks to its large internal market and its relatively high level of product regulations (especially with regard to environmental protection), was able to influence rules beyond its borders (Vogel 1995). Ian Manners (2002) subsequently coined the term 'normative power Europe' to make sense of the European Union's role in the world, which is largely built on its ability to change perceptions of what is normal in world affairs. His seminal article on the subject was recognised by then European Commission President Barroso as one of the most influential works on the EU of the previous decade, testifying to the hold it had on EU officials' self-perception. More recently, Chad Damro has argued that 'the EU may be best understood as a *market power Europe* that exercises its power through the externalization of economic and social market-related policies and regulatory measures' (2012: 682, emphasis added). This power is determined by the size of the EU's market and its institutional abilities to adopt and externalise ambitious rules, together with the support of interest groups to spread norms globally.

EU officials have, for some time, been conscious of the Union's ability to export its rules, values and model abroad. In 2005, the European Commission published a Communication on 'European Values in a Globalised World', where it explicitly differentiated the 'European model' from others in the rest of the world, including the US, and noted that 'European citizens have greater expectations of the state than their equivalents in Asia or America' (European Commission 2005: 4). In 2007, in a document on the external dimension of the Single Market, the European Commission (2007b: 2, 5, 8) wrote that, '[i]n many areas [...] the EU is looked upon as a regulatory leader and standard-setter', with the Single Market being 'a tool to foster high quality rules and standards'. It also identified 'a window of opportunity to push global solutions forward'.

However, with the crisis and increasing competition from emerging markets, this confidence seems to have waned in recent years, in many ways paving the way for greater transatlantic cooperation. The focus in Europe has increasingly moved away from 'exporting rules' towards the imperatives of boosting 'competitiveness', which had already become an ever more central concept in EU policymaking since the 2000 Lisbon Agenda and its reinvigoration in the middle of the decade. In the EU's Single Market Act of 2010, the Single Market was perceived less as an instrument to set global rules and more as a 'base camp that allows European businesses to prepare themselves better for international competition and the conquest of new markets' (European Commission 2010a: 17). As an NGO campaigner remarked sharply in 2013, 'the political priority has gone from saving the planet to saving your job' (Milevska 2013).

The crisis has indeed hit the EU hard, not only in purely

economic terms but also when it comes to how policymakers perceive the EU's position in the world. As is written in the preface of the successor to the Lisbon Agenda, the new overarching ten-year strategy for the EU entitled 'Europe 2020', '[t]he crisis is a wake-up call, the moment where we recognise that "business as usual" would consign us to a gradual decline, to the second rank of the new global order' (European Commission 2010b: 2). EU leaders' vision since the crisis is increasingly that the continent has to become more competitive to survive, and thrive, in the 'global race'. What in the previous decade were still seen, with some pride, as distinctive futures of the European model are now often depicted as an unaffordable drag on European competitiveness. A mantra tirelessly repeated during the past years, first by Angela Merkel and later by other EU leaders, is that the EU has 7 per cent of the world's population, 25 per cent of its GDP and 50 per cent of its social spending (cited in *The Economist* 2013). The implication of these statistics is that the Union can no longer be this generous or it will lose in its competition with emerging economies. EU policymakers should stop being naïve in believing that the emerging powers will keep adopting the EU's lofty rules and values, it is argued. The distinctive 'European social model' has thus been reduced to a burden borne by the EU in the global economic race.

A large number of influential decision-makers in the EU are thus of the opinion that, while the EU may have written some of the rules for globalisation for a brief period in the first decade of the twenty-first century, its reign is now over. It can no longer afford to have more generous and stringent social, environmental and public health rules. It is of course undeniable that the relative global market sizes of both the EU and the US are shrinking because of the rise of emerging economies. As a result, politicians across the Atlantic look at China as a key contender for global economic and political leadership. Whereas the shares of global imports of the US and the EU in 2002 amounted to 25.7 per cent and 18.9 per cent respectively (44.6 per cent in total), this had decreased a decade later to 16.2 per cent and 16 per cent (or 32.2 per cent on aggregate). Over the same period, China's share of global imports almost doubled, from 6.3 per cent to 12.6 per cent (Eurostat 2015).

In such a context of rapidly declining economic leverage, the reasoning is that the US and the EU 'need to maximize [their] influence by sticking together' (De Gucht 2014a). This view is fully shared by the new EU Commissioner for Trade, the Swedish liberal Cecilia Malmström. In her confirmation hearing before the European Parliament, she noted that 'there is a strategic dimension to the regulatory work [in TTIP]. If the world's two biggest powers when it comes to trade manage to agree standards, these would be the basis for international cooperation to create global standards' (cited in European Parliament 2014: 8). Similar statements have also been made on the American side. For example, US President Obama declared in his 2015 State of the Union address that, 'as we speak, China wants to write the rules for the world's fastest-growing region. . . . Why would we let that happen? We should write those rules' (White House 2015; see also White House 2013b). The US's acute concern with the rise of China, which has led (among other things) to its 'pivot to Asia', has meant that TPP and TTIP have explicitly been seen as a way of containing China economically. This is an even more aggressive version of the geo-economic rationale than that usually articulated by EU leaders.

To sum up, a central argument for advocates of TTIP has been the ability to set joint global standards in the face of the rise of China (and other emerging powers). This narrative is in line with the perception, especially persistent in the EU after the crisis, that European and American market power is declining. It has led to a remarkable redefinition of the relationship between the EU and the US when it comes to regulatory values and culture. In the first years of this millennium, there was a lot of emphasis on the unique 'European model' as distinct from more *laissez-faire* visions of capitalism in the US, especially with regard to the responsibility of the state, tax and social policies, and the role of the precautionary principle in environmental and health policies. This unique model had to be protected in the face of globalisation through a distinctive trade policy aimed at 'managing globalisation' (a term coined by then EU Trade Commissioner Pascal Lamy), often against the US view of more unfettered globalisation (Jacoby and Meunier 2010).

In the meantime, the emphasis on differences between the EU and the US has given way to stressing the fundamental similarities between values and policy models across the Atlantic to make transatlantic cooperation seem more natural. This shift from highlighting paradigmatic difference to fundamental similarity when it comes to EU and US regulatory values and models is not only a key discursive tool to counter criticisms of transatlantic regulatory convergence. It is also a necessary stepping-stone in the construction of the narrative that the EU and the US can agree on 'setting global standards'.

However, we show in the remainder of this chapter that, even if (for the sake of argument) the EU and the US can succeed in overcoming regulatory differences, this will not automatically lead to the establishment of global standards. There are different ways to achieve regulatory alignment, and these have very different consequences.

Regulatory cooperation: the devil is in the mode

This is not the place to write an extensive history of the international trade regime or to explain in an elaborate manner when and why regulatory barriers came onto the agenda. We will address these issues at greater length in chapter 3. Suffice to draw the reader's attention to what is known in the literature as the 'reef theory'. An analogy is drawn here between traditional trade barriers such as tariffs and quotas (the 'sea level') and other, so-called NTBs or 'behind-the-border barriers' (the 'reefs'). Reefs have become increasingly visible because obstacles to international trade – the sea level – have been lowered after successive rounds of multilateral trade agreements (under the GATT/WTO) have reduced tariffs to historical lows and abolished quota restrictions. In the 1970s, non-tariff barriers were still understood in a rather limited way as barriers to trade that were not tariffs but had a similar, explicit intention to restrict trade, such as countervailing or anti-dumping duties, voluntary export restraints or direct subsidies to enterprises. Increasingly, the term 'non-tariff barrier' has come to cover regulations whose primary objective is not to restrict trade but which serve other potentially legitimate policy goals, such as, for example, health, consumer or environmental protection. As we will discuss in the next chapter, non-tariff barriers have not simply been 'discovered' because of a natural lowering of the sea level. The concept was in large part also manufactured by a 'redefinition of the common sense concept of "trade barrier"' (Lang 2011: 224).

Differences in regulations that prescribe specific product or service requirements, or regulate the way a product or service is produced and/or delivered, have often been identified over the past decades as the most important remaining obstacles to international trade. This also applies to the transatlantic trade relationship. As the impact assessment preparing the ground for the TTIP negotiations states, 'regulatory measures constitute the greatest obstacle to increased trade and investment between the EU and the US, identified in numerous studies and surveys and public consultations, as well as by way of anecdotal evidence' (European Commission 2013a: 17).

How can states deal with these differences in regulations while trying to limit the negative effects this has on trade? One of the general trading rules of the WTO – this also applies to regulations – is known as 'national treatment'; states are free to decide which regulations to apply, but they have to apply these in a non-discriminatory fashion to all providers, be they foreign or domestic. The WTO's TBT and SPS agreements include a number of other, mostly procedural, prescriptions for adopting regulatory measures, but the EU and the US have clearly stated that their intention is to go much further in TTIP and 'eliminate regulatory divergence' to a significant extent. However, they have not yet specified clearly *how* this will be realised. Nonetheless, this is crucial for the geo-economic justification of TTIP.

If states want to go the extra mile with regard to regulatory cooperation, going beyond national treatment, they have two principal options (with some further distinctions we develop below): either a 'harmonisation' of their erstwhile different rules or simply a 'mutual recognition' of existing rules (which remain distinct). In the case of harmonisation (mode 1 in table 2.1), regulatory 'diversity is overcome by finding a common denominator' (Schmidt 2007: 261). If the EU and the US have different requirements, for instance, for headlights, bumpers or seat belts for cars (an example the European Commission is wont to use), they could decide, in future, simply to apply either the EU's rules or those of the US or jointly to adopt an international standard – perhaps from UNECE (as has been suggested in the case of motor vehicles). However, as a close reading of position papers by the European Commission suggests, and as has been confirmed in a number of interviews we conducted with policymakers,[2] the harmonisation approach cannot be expected to be adopted widely, if at all, in TTIP. On its Q&A webpage about the agreement, the Commission is very explicit about this: 'harmonisation is not on the agenda' (European Commission 2015f). The reason is that it is seen as (politically) very difficult and administratively cumbersome for negotiators to agree for each and every regulation which party's rules may be superior and will be adopted by the other side, or to recognise that both have in the past been applying standards that are inferior to an already existing international regulation that will henceforth be applied. Moreover, the outcome of harmonisation towards one of the parties' existing rule or standard is seen as zero-sum from a political economy perspective: only one of the parties has to suffer the complete adaptation cost, while the other has to bear none.

It is therefore more likely that the approach to be followed will be one of mutual recognition.[3] This mode of regulatory cooperation can be defined as 'creating conditions under which participating parties commit to the principle that if a product or service can be sold lawfully in one jurisdiction, it can be sold lawfully in any other participating jurisdiction' (Nicolaïdis and Shaffer 2005: 264). Under this approach, the EU and the US would keep their diverging car safety standards for bumpers or seat belts, but they would formally recognise that these parts of their regulatory systems for motor vehicles are broadly the same in terms of their impact on safety. This mode has the practical advantage of avoiding having to have both parties agree about which standard is superior and of thus burdening one side with the adjustment costs. But, while mutual recognition might be preferable from a negotiator's point of view, there are a number of problems that may arise from adopting such a mode of regulatory convergence.

The approaches to regulatory alignment we have discussed above differ fundamentally when it comes to their vision of, and hence the consequences for, the state–market relationship.[4] With national treatment (the status quo), there is the primacy of (national) politics, insofar as governments have considerable freedom to set standards that will serve a public policy purpose. With mutual recognition, there is the primacy of the market, insofar as firms have the choice of which standard they choose to comply with. Finally, with harmonisation, political governance over the market is reinstated at the supranational level, with a new standard being determined as a result of a political negotiation. As a result, Joel Trachtman (2007: 783) argues that '[mutual] recognition is by its nature purely deregulatory', insofar as it allows firms to bypass higher standards. He therefore notes that mutual recognition can be desirable only when underpinned by essential harmonisation, where a minimum standard is agreed, as within the EU's Single Market. We discuss the implications for levels of risk protection and democratic decision-making of different approaches to regulatory cooperation more elaborately in chapter 3. In the remainder of this chapter, however, we turn to the question of how the choice of mode of regulatory cooperation affects the ability of the EU and the US jointly to 'set global standards'.

We therefore have to make some further subtle but significant distinctions. Firstly, parties to regulatory cooperation agreements can decide not to go as far as really recognizing each other's *substantial* standards and accept that their differences in actual standards are legitimate and reasonable. They may still agree, however, that it is unnecessarily costly for exporters to have their products tested doubly – not only in their home country but also in the country of destination. In that case, they could decide to let the differences in substantial standards exist but to mutually recognise each other's *conformity testing* procedures and bodies (mode 4 in table 2.1).

Alternatively, they could go a step further and decide to mutually recognise each other's substantial standards (as in the example given above for car safety). Again, this can be done in two different ways. The benefits of mutual recognition can be extended to the rest of the world, meaning that all exporters to

Table 2.1 Modes of regulatory cooperation and TTIP

	1 Harmonisation	Mutual recognition		
		Of regulations		Of conformity testing
		2 *Erga omnes*	3 Bilateral	4 Of conformity testing
Probability of being reached in TTIP	Ruled out	Low	Moderate for a number of sectors	High in a number of sectors
Potential for setting global standards	High	Medium	Low	None
Effect on domestic standards	Potential for race to the top*	High potential for race to the bottom	Moderate potential for race to the bottom	Limited

More ambitious ⟶ Less ambitious

Note: *However, harmonisation does not guarantee a race-to-the-top dynamic. This would happen only if both parties were to agree to adopt the highest standard, be it an existing US, EU or international standard or a new, more ambitious standard.

the EU and the US would profit from having to comply with only one of the TTIP partners' regulations to access both markets. This is what is called *erga omnes* mutual recognition (mode 2 in table 2.1) and is how the EU's Single Market works – countering fears among third countries during the late 1980s that its completion ('Europe 1992') would result in a protectionist 'Fortress Europe' (see Hanson 1998).

In contrast, the benefits of mutual recognition could be limited to suppliers located in either party in what is known as *bilateral* mutual recognition (mode 3 in table 2.1). In this case, a car produced in the EU according to EU safety regulations could be marketed in the US without having to undergo adaptations to US standards. But this market access advantage would not be extended to suppliers from outside the EU (or from outside the US in the case of the EU market). It would imply a cost reduction for EU and US car manufacturers with sales on the other side of the Atlantic, but it would not grant the same advantage to third-country producers. Outsiders would even be at a competitive disadvantage, as they would have to keep producing different car models meeting different regulatory requirements, while their EU and US competitors would be exempted from that burden.

While the negotiators have not communicated in detail as to how they are pursuing regulatory cooperation for different sectors, based on what is written in position papers and interviews we have conducted,[5] we argue that it is reasonable to expect that, for those sectors where substantial regulatory convergence is pursued, bilateral mutual recognition will be the chosen approach. The EU has stated its preference for that mode because it makes regulatory cooperation more attractive for those sectors that hope to gain from regulatory cooperation while limiting the costs for those sectors that stand to lose from real regulatory alignment. For the car sector, one of the largest beneficiaries of an ambitious comprehensive agreement according to the European Commission's impact assessment, the Commission notes that 'it can be reasonably assumed that in reality the outcome of negotiations on the NTMs [non-tariff measures] . . . would *rather result in bilateral than in erga omnes recognition* of safety standards; . . . [in that case] the positive effect on output in the car sector could even be bigger', because only EU firms would get easier access to the US market but not others, and *vice versa* (European Commission 2013a: 43, emphasis added). The Commission arrives at the same conclusion for the electrical machinery sector, which stands to lose considerably from TTIP. Seeking to assuage fears, it states that 'the expected approach to be followed in the negotiations with the US would focus on regulatory coherence and a degree of mutual recognition between the EU and the US standards' without entailing 'spillover effects to third countries'. Increased competition through improved market access would be limited to US firms and not apply to the rest of the world (ibid.: 41).

Analysing statements on how regulatory cooperation will be pursued in TTIP (a task that requires proficiency in 'the art of reading footnotes') reveals that *mutual recognition* is much likelier to result than *harmonisation*, and that this is to apply *bilaterally* rather than *erga omnes*. As we will see in chapter 3, this choice corresponds to the preference of multinational enterprises that are active on both sides of the Atlantic and risks unleashing a deregulatory dynamic. But, here, the crucial conclusion to draw is that bilateral mutual recognition does not provide added incentives for third-country firms to adopt EU/US standards, as doing so would offer no additional advantages vis-à-vis the status quo.

TTIP is unlikely to lead to global standards

The more (the economic rationale for) TTIP has been criticised over the past two years, the more its advocates have put forward a geo-economic and geopolitical rationale. This is often directed at more progressive critics, promising them the possibility of establishing high global standards while also invoking the gloomy prospect of having to conform to Chinese rule(s) if TTIP is not concluded. However, in this chapter we have shown that TTIP does not automatically translate into prolonged economic leadership for the EU and the US. What is more, the agreement may even accelerate the decline in regulatory leadership of both entities, and of the EU in particular.

The probability that TTIP will generate 'transatlantic regulatory power' depends on the modalities of the agreement and, more specifically, on the mode of regulatory cooperation. A harmonised standard – where one and the same standard is jointly agreed – stands the highest chance of being adopted by third countries and, thus, of becoming a true global rule. But the negotiators have indicated that this is not a feasible outcome of the negotiations in most areas. *Erga omnes* mutual recognition, which we have argued is also less likely to be used, could similarly provide an attractive incentive for third countries to align their regulations with those of the EU or the US, because this would immediately provide them access to the other party's market.

However, if the EU and the US choose only to mutually recognise each other's rules *bilaterally*, as we argue is most likely, this will not incentivise third countries to align their standards with transatlantic ones. It would mean that third countries' enterprises will not enjoy the advantages of TTIP, and consequently they will have little or no reason to change their current practices (or to lobby their governments to align their regulations). On the contrary, they stand to be disadvantaged competitively vis-à-vis firms located on both sides of the Atlantic and might ultimately lose their presence on the transatlantic market. As a result, trade diversion may occur (for the impact of this on developing countries, see Rollo et al. 2013); suppliers from outside the transatlantic region would lose market share here to EU and US competitors and may therefore shift their exports elsewhere. This comes on top of the trade diversion resulting from bilateral tariff elimination. This may make it less, rather than more, likely that third countries would align their regulations with those of the EU and/or the US. The transatlantic partners would thus stand to lose instead of gain market power because of TTIP.

Mutual recognition may also impact negatively on global regulatory leadership in a second way, even if it were to be applied *erga omnes*. In cases where there are significant differences between current EU and US standards, third-country firms could simply conform to the least costly standard and enjoy free access to the other market. For the entity with the higher current level of protection, this would mean losing influence over third countries' regulatory practices when compared to the current state of play, as it would feel the pressure of competition from all firms opting for the lower standard. Given that EU standards are generally (if not always; see chapter 3) more stringent, this would see the EU lose comparatively more leverage than the US.

Thirdly, TTIP may also undermine the EU's soft power as the supposed distinctiveness of its economic and regulatory model, much applauded during the mid-2000s, is diluted (see Defraigne 2013). This would be not just the consequence of a TTIP deal with substantial regulatory convergence provisions but already follows from the broader discourse invoked by advocates of a transatlantic trade deal which emphasises shared EU and US values (and, more concretely, regulatory goals, systems and outcomes) and the threat posed by China as an emerging regulatory power.

It is a mistake to assume that TTIP will automatically lead to the 'setting of global standards' by the EU and the US, thereby containing the rise of China. However, the narrative that the transatlantic alliance should leave behind the quarrels of earlier days to avoid being relegated in the global order is useful to convince people that it is not transatlantic regulatory cooperation but its absence that is something to fear. This brings us to the key dimension and objective of TTIP, on which we focus in the following chapter: bridging regulatory differences and cutting red tape.

3

The Bottom Line:
Cutting Red Tape

Having shown that it is unlikely that TTIP will lead to a spec-
tacular 'growth and jobs' boost or contribute to global economic
leadership for the EU and the US, in this chapter we examine what
might instead be expected from it. Why is all of this effort being
put into the negotiations?

We do not share some of the most vocal critics' view that TTIP
will allow US corporate interests (and a fifth column of EU multinationals) to ram hormone-treated beef, chlorinated chicken
and genetically modified vegetables down European consumers'
throats or to privatise the UK National Health Service (NHS) at the
stroke of a pen. On the former, the EU and the US have already
been engaged in a number of highly politicised trade disputes at
the WTO, which have failed to alter EU regulations substantially
on account of the institutionally entrenched nature of the 'precautionary principle' in a highly controversial area. Meanwhile,

the services liberalisation commitments seen in TTIP are largely about 'locking in' existing levels of marketisation in public services rather than bringing about a privatisation from above (Raza 2014).

The effects of TTIP are thus likely to be much subtler, if not unimportant, entrenching institutional machineries and processes that are likely to have a deregulatory impact. While close scrutiny of the negotiations by public advocacy groups has led to a softening of the real bite that the regulatory cooperation commitments may have, TTIP's main consequence is expected to be a reinforcement of economistic disciplines in decision-making. In other words, it may lead to the effects of regulatory proposals being increasingly judged against their consequences for trade, competitiveness and economic growth. What is being proposed in the agreement is thus still largely in line with the preferences of businesses on both sides of the Atlantic seeking to reduce their costs by minimising not only barriers to transatlantic trade but also the impact of domestic rules and regulations. Crucially, TTIP's focus on cutting 'red tape', as the agreement's advocates often call regulations, dovetails with initiatives in the EU to go over rules with a fine-tooth comb. As Colin Crouch (2014: 2) argues, 'a trade treaty with the US seems to be reinforcing pressures already at work within Europe, rather than some distinctively American threat.'

We begin this chapter by providing some context to the regulatory cooperation negotiations at the heart of TTIP. One of the most important ways in which the neoliberal sway in economic thinking and practice since the late 1970s has also affected the trade regime is the uncritical acceptance of the premise that a wide array of domestic policies are in fact 'non-tariff barriers'. While TTIP has been seen as a 'game-changer' (in many respects with good reason), there is considerable continuity between these negotiations and broader trends in global trade politics. We then briefly compare the regulatory systems in the EU and the US that negotiators are seeking to reconcile and discuss proposals for regulatory cooperation in TTIP. These have strongly reflected the preferences of business organisations in the EU and the US, especially their advocacy of mutual recognition, horizontal disciplines and coordinative institutions for regulatory policies as the way to reduce regulatory differences. However, as opposition to TTIP has gained strength, negotiators have been forced to reassure the public by softening the ambitions for regulatory cooperation. Nonetheless, we argue that, while negotiators may have promised that TTIP will not lead to lowering levels of protection in the EU and the US directly, the procedural disciplines and institutions for regulatory decision-making that may be negotiated – and the increased competition that transatlantic liberalisation would entail by definition[1] – would still constitute a further constraint on public policy decisions. The whole focus on 'cutting red tape' in TTIP is very much in line with a similar contemporary agenda of 'better regulation' *within* the EU. This is also how we interpret the provisions on ISDS, which are likely to lead to regulatory chill in policymaking. TTIP should be seen as an attempt to further guard the market from political interference, even if the level of political opposition to the agreement has meant that it has not been entirely successful so far.

Regulation in the crosshairs of the global trade regime

TTIP is the culmination of a broader process where international trade negotiations increasingly intrude on domestic policy autonomy, a trend that goes back nearly four decades. Just as the launch of the TTIP negotiations has often been framed as a response to the most recent crisis, an important qualitative leap in the global trade regime was supposedly taken in reaction to the 1970s oil shock and stagflation crisis. As Andrew Lang has written, in his discussion of the shift from 'embedded liberalism' (this term is from Ruggie 1982) to neoliberalism in the global trade regime,

> by the beginning of the 1970s the GATT had been used to challenge only a highly restricted range of internal regulatory measures which affected international trade in a direct and obviously discriminatory way. By the end of the 1990s, however, as informal norms limiting the scope of application of GATT regulatory disciplines were gradually reconstituted, the range of measures subject to challenge . . . had broadened considerably. (Lang 2011: 223)

After first resorting without apparent success to protectionist policies, the response to the 1970s crises was to pursue further and deeper liberalisation through regional integration and the multilateral trading system. This would eventually lead to the completion of the Single Market in the European Union (1992) and NAFTA in North America (1994). At the multilateral level, the GATT Tokyo Round agreement, concluded in 1979, tackled non-tariff measures for the first time in a series of 'codes'. Later, the subsequent Uruguay Round agreement (1994) established not only the WTO, which featured a reinforced dispute settlement mechanism, but also a number of agreements focusing on behind-the-border issues, such as services regulations (the General Agreement on Trade in Services, or GATS), technical and food safety measures (the Agreements on TBT and SPS) and intellectual property rights (the Agreement on Trade-Related Intellectual Property Rights, or TRIPS). On a fundamental level, what shifted in this period is the perception of what constitutes a barrier to trade. This was no longer seen as limited to deliberately discriminatory measures but was broadened to potentially encompass every governmental action that supposedly distorts

> the conditions of competition between foreign and domestic products, as compared to the conditions of competition which would exist in an *imagined 'free' market*. . . . The result is that the notion of a 'trade distortion' comes to be equated in practice with the existence of a commercially significant institution or regulatory *difference* between countries. (Lang 2011: 226–7, emphasis added)

This is exactly the way remaining trade barriers are seen in TTIP, where negotiators on both sides have stressed time and again that the 'most important [area of the negotiations is]: reducing regulatory *differences* to facilitate trade' (De Gucht 2014b, emphasis added). Domestic regulatory differences between the EU and the US have been redefined as non-tariff barriers, or alternatively as 'red tape', with the focus being on their economic, quantifiable effects, not just among modellers, as we saw in chapter 1, but also among policymakers. Such a framing can have a significant impact on whether the intrusion of trade negotiations into domestic policies is seen as acceptable. It is much easier for citizens and voters to accept regulatory commitments in trade agreements when these are presented as 'cutting red tape' rather than as reciprocal concessions on health protection measures. Redefining regulations as barriers or red tape is thus a significant political act that can help in 'manufacturing consent' for unpopular policy decisions (Herman and Chomsky 1988).

As we will see in the remainder of this chapter, this depiction of differences in regulation as non-tariff barriers, and the intention of addressing them in TTIP through mutual recognition and increased disciplines and cooperation in the preparation of future regulation, is very much in line with the preferences of transatlantic big business. Before we discuss these issues, however, we provide a very brief overview of the main differences between the regulatory regimes in the EU and the US.

Regulatory politics in the EU and the US

Regulation in the EU and the US differs not only in terms of its outcomes but also when it comes to the process by which rules are made. This is one of the reasons why, notwithstanding many attempts at transatlantic regulatory cooperation, this has proven largely elusive (see the Introduction). As we will see in the remainder of this chapter, TTIP is meant to kill two birds with one stone: by reducing the differences in the *process* by which regulations are made (under the heading of 'horizontal cooperation'), it is also intended to make convergence of regulatory *outcomes* easier ('sectoral cooperation').

EU and US regulatory politics are different in a number of ways (see Alemanno 2014). While the Constitution mandates that the US Congress has the sole power to make laws, in practice there are over 100 federal agencies (such as the Food and Drug Administration [FDA], the Occupational Safety and Health Administration [OSHA] or the Environmental Protection Agency [EPA]) with a remit allowing them to pass rules or regulations in a certain field and which have the effect of laws. Congress only generally instructs and exercises broad oversight of those agencies. In the EU, regulations can be set directly either by the legislature (the European Parliament and Council, after an initiative by the Commission through what is called the 'Ordinary Legislative Procedure') or by the European Commission via its competence to draft delegated and implementing acts, subject to case-by-case oversight by Member States in the Council (and sometimes also the European Parliament). Hence, the role of (directly) politically accountable actors in the day-to-day regulatory process is much stronger in the EU than in the US, where risk assessment *and* risk management is delegated to non-majoritarian agencies. With regard to standardisation, specifically, defining the technical standards for goods and services (such as the shape and size of light bulbs), the process in the EU has been characterised as a centralised public system, while in the US it has been defined as decentralised, with the private sector playing a key role in defining the standards (see CEN/CENELEC 2013).

Secondly, the involvement of the private sector in regulatory policymaking is considered stronger in the US. Under the

Administrative Procedure Act, it has a 'notice-and-comment' system requiring all agency proposals that carry the force and effect of law to go through a profound stakeholder consultation process. This especially gives business organisations with the appropriate means and expertise at their disposal the opportunity to engage in lobbying on regulatory proposals. Moreover, in the US, the Office of Information and Regulatory Affairs (OIRA) is in charge of reviewing whether proposed rules meet a number of requirements, such as being based on the best available science; being drafted in a process involving public participation; being the least burdensome alternative available; and being based on a cost–benefit analysis. This agency has been accused by NGOs such as Public Citizen (2013) both of delaying new regulations in the US and for upholding a deregulatory bias when reviewing regulations (see also Steinzor 2012). These procedural requirements are also subject to judicial review.

Thirdly, while impact assessments have increasingly become the norm in the EU, they are a much less strict formal requirement, with their parameters prescribed in far less detail. There does not have to be a (legally enforceable) link between the impact assessment and the outcome of the regulatory process. A study by the European Commission's DG for Enterprise and Industry in 2007 referred to the US's binding IA approach as 'quantitative economic analysis', while that of the EU was characterised as 'an integrated approach, which establishes no ranking between economic, social and environmental impacts of policy options' (O'Connor Close and Mancini 2007: 4).[2] This is of course also related to the impact of the 'precautionary principle' (the ability to rapidly protect human, animal or plant health and the environment where scientific data for risk evaluation may be incomplete) in the EU, which is enshrined in Article 191 of the Treaty on the Functioning of the EU. The precautionary principle hence enables regulators to take into account information and considerations other than strict scientific and economic cost-benefit analysis when managing risks (see Bergkamp and Kogan 2013).

The implications of all this for the TTIP negotiations are that regulatory cooperation faces the challenge of reconciling rather different administrative systems. Another consequence is that, in the decentralised system in the US, it is less self-evident that commitments made by the federal government will be followed up by the hundreds of agencies with regulatory or standard-setting competencies. This risk of domestic non-compliance by decentralised agencies is one of the reasons why the US is hesitant to go into sectoral agreements in the TTIP negotiations and was responsible for the failure to implement most of the EU–US MRAs of the late 1990s. Aside from these practical considerations, the attempt to reconcile these two rather different regulatory systems has some more fundamental consequences for the nature of domestic policymaking. It is to these that we turn in the remainder of this chapter.

In sum, the EU's regulatory system is seen as still adhering more to the principle of the primacy of politics (where democratically generated societal preferences trump scientific considerations in the risk management decision) and to precautionary and hazard-based ('the potential for a substance, activity or process to cause harm or adverse effect'; Lofsted 2011: 149) than to stricter risk-based analysis ('a combination of the likelihood and the severity of a substance, activity or process to cause harm'; ibid.). On the whole, the opposite goes for the US. As we will discuss in what follows, the EU's regulatory system has in the past decade been undergoing some changes that are bringing it closer to that of the US (see also Meuwese 2011), a process TTIP may well expedite.[3] In the next section, we show how TTIP's focus on and approach to regulatory convergence is very much in line with the preferences of big business organisations, before discussing how an internal reform process is already bringing EU regulatory policies closer to those of the US.

The business agenda on TTIP

Business interests, especially the larger, multinational firms that are active across borders, are represented, among others, by BUSINESSEUROPE (a supranational confederation of European employers' organisations) and by the US Chamber of Commerce. These organisations, and their largest members, have a history of cooperating to weigh in on issues of transatlantic economic interest, such as through the Transatlantic Business Dialogue (TABD) that was convened in 1995 by the US Department of Commerce and the European Commission (Cowles 2001: 168–70). They have been lobbying for profound regulatory cooperation and convergence for years and could build on this work in their TTIP activities. In the meantime, BUSINESSEUROPE and the US Chamber of Commerce, together with a number of other organisations,[4] have launched the 'Business Alliance for a Transatlantic

Trade and Investment Partnership' to 'educate and advocate for the successful conclusion of TTIP' (BUSINESSEUROPE et al. 2013).

BUSINESSEUROPE and the US Chamber of Commerce had already clearly conveyed their preferences for the negotiations months before these were officially announced in President Obama's 2013 State of the Union address. The resemblance of these organisations' positions with the eventual official agenda for TTIP is striking, especially their call for mutual recognition and horizontal regulatory cooperation commitments (BUSINESSEUROPE and US Chamber of Commerce 2012). These two peak associations of course do not have a monopoly on representing businesses in the EU and the US. Other organisations have also participated in consultations with policymakers. In this vein, Alasdair Young (2013) has undertaken an analysis of the submissions made by business organisations to the joint EU–US consultation on regulatory issues organised by the High Level Working Group on Jobs and Growth (HLWG) in October 2012. He found that mutual recognition is by far the preferred form of regulatory cooperation among transatlantic business coalitions (composed largely of multinational firms) as well as by most of the 'peak' associations in the US and the EU. Big business on both sides of the Atlantic is on the same page. Only in agriculture, the least transnational of all sectors, is there a clear diverging preference for harmonisation based on home rules. The US agro-associations object to the EU's use of the precautionary principle and demand that the EU switch to a 'sound science' approach to risk management. Andreas Dür and Lisa Lechner (2015) have found very similar results using a larger sample of business submissions, position papers and speeches on TTIP. They also conclude that the trade policy positions of the EU and the US largely reflect those business interests.

With regard to aligning the regulatory *processes* in the EU and the US, business organisations on both sides have for long argued that 'common regulatory methodologies should be created in the long run' (AmCham EU 2008: 1). On the EU side, business organisations have also advocated that the EU should move towards the US practice of strict cost–benefit analysis and 'should give due weight to the burden anticipated for affected companies' (BDI 2008: 4). The German Industry Association has even gone as far as to suggest that 'US and EU regulatory authorities should consider a common threshold for determining when to cancel or modify regulatory plans based on the net cost generated by the cost–benefit analysis' (ibid.).

The final report of the HLWG that led to the decision to open negotiations on TTIP lists five basic components a TTIP agreement should contain (which is in line with the business position detailed just now). It foresees an SPS-plus component (in other words, an agreement on SPS that goes beyond existing WTO disciplines in this area in terms of, for example, scientific risk assessment in food safety); a TBT-plus component (going beyond WTO disciplines with regard to, for example, reducing unnecessary burdens arising from differences in conformity assessment requirements); sectoral annexes with detailed commitments for specific goods and services sectors; cross-cutting disciplines on regulatory coherence and transparency; and a framework for regulatory cooperation in the future.[5]

On the latter issues, the initial position paper of the European

Commission on 'Trade cross-cutting disciplines and institutional provisions' (European Commission 2013c), written before the intense public debate on the negotiations kicked off, reveals the level of ambition that was present at the start of the negotiations. The horizontal disciplines on the regulatory process should apply to 'all measures of general application . . . regardless of the level at which they are adopted and of the body which adopts them' (ibid.: 2). The horizontal rules and the regulatory cooperation commitments are seen as intermediate steps towards 'the ultimate goal [of] a more integrated transatlantic market where goods produced and services originating in one party in accordance with its regulatory requirements could be marketed in the other without adaptation' (ibid.: 3), an explicit reference to the final objective of creating a single market (analogous to the European one) based on the principle of mutual recognition. However, negotiators already recognised at this stage that this objective could not be realised in one fell swoop. TTIP would act as an intermediate step and contain procedural commitments that would oblige the EU and the US to consult better and cooperate when developing regulations (agreeing on regulatory principles, best practices and transparency), to strengthen the assessment of impacts of regulations on international trade and investment flows, and to use common or similar criteria and methods in executing impact assessments. TTIP would become a 'living agreement' that facilitates regulatory cooperation beyond its formal conclusion. This would be the task of the regulatory institutional framework, whose main components would be (at this point it is worth reproducing the Commission's original position paper at length):

- A consultation procedure to discuss and address issues arising with respect to EU or US regulations or regulatory initiatives, at the request of either party.
- A streamlined procedure to amend the sectoral annexes of TTIP or to add new ones, through a simplified mechanism *not entailing domestic ratification procedures*.
- A body with regulatory competences (a regulatory cooperation council or committee), assisted by sectoral working groups, as appropriate, which could be charged with overseeing implementation of the regulatory provisions of the TTIP and make recommendations to the body with decision-making power under TTIP. This regulatory cooperation body would for example examine concrete proposals on how to enhance greater compatibility/convergence, including through recognition of equivalence of regulations, mutual recognition, etc. (Ibid.: 5, emphasis added)

One of the more revealing passages in this document (italicised above) is the idea that an eventual regulatory cooperation body would be able to amend the agreement without domestic ratification. Such strong language was, however, quickly criticised both by NGOs (e.g., CEO 2013c) and by sovereignty-sensitive politicians (*EU Trade Insights* 2015). Consequently, when this position paper was translated into a textual proposal from the EU for the negotiations, the wording was toned down. It now stated that 'the RCB [regulatory cooperation body] will not have the power to adopt legal acts' (European Commission 2015a: 11). The scope of the horizontal disciplines has also been limited somewhat, applying in a more confined way to the non-central level (see

European Commission 2015g). But, while the scope and bite of the horizontal disciplines have been moderated to some extent, these procedures would still strengthen commercial interests in deciding on the priorities for regulation (what should be regulated) and give such interests more weight when considering the cost and benefits of alternative solutions (how these risks should be regulated).

The extent to which the EU's initial ideas for the regulatory dimension of TTIP are a 'copy/paste' of businesses' demands is remarkable. But both negotiators and their supporters in business organisations argue that it is not only businesses that stand to gain from TTIP, and regulatory cooperation in particular, but also consumers (e.g., American Chambers of Commerce to the European Union 2014: 15), analogous in some ways to the claim that it is not just big business but also SMEs who benefit from TTIP (see chapters 1 and 4). Consumers are often depicted in academic and political debates as the losers of 'collective action' dynamics when it comes to trade policy (see Olson 1965). As a diffuse interest that benefits from liberalisation through cheaper prices and greater product choice, they are said to fail to mobilise in contrast to concentrated losers from trade liberalisation, who will usually lobby for protection.

However, in both the EU and the US there *are* consumer organisations that mobilise on trade politics and have voiced views that are mostly critical of TTIP. In the EU, the Bureau of European Union Consumer Organisations (BEUC) is the well-respected umbrella group for forty national consumer organisations from thirty-one European countries, while in the US there are a larger number of consumer organisations with different priorities and strategies. Consumer organisations are also organised across the Atlantic in the Transatlantic Consumer Dialogue (TACD). In one of its position papers on the negotiations, after expressing general support for balanced, conditional trade liberalisation, BEUC writes under the heading of 'Non-Tariff Barriers (NTBs) and regulatory coherence' that

> [i]t is essential for negotiators to acknowledge that *consumer protection laws may not be interpreted as trading rules*, but are there to benefit the society as a whole. . . . The focus on reducing non-tariff barriers inevitably therefore raises *concerns about the deal being used as a backdoor mechanism to reduce protections*, or to harmonise by levelling down. (BEUC 2014a: 5–6, emphasis added)

The Transatlantic Consumer Dialogue has taken a very similar position on TTIP (TACD 2013). Consumer organisations are thus not only more vocal than is commonly assumed; they are also less convinced about the one-sided focus on cost-reduction that business organisations and negotiators single out as one of the principal gains from TTIP. Instead, what the likes of BEUC and the TACD have done is draw attention to the benefits of regulation (see also Myant and O'Brien 2015). As we will argue in the next section, they have good reasons to be suspicious of deregulation through the back door in the case of TTIP. Regulation in the EU is currently already being scrutinised internally according to similar logics, arguments and concepts. There is a strong parallel between the regulatory cooperation commitments being discussed in the TTIP negotiations and the review of regulations and the regulatory processes currently ongoing within the

EU. This has been applauded by the US ambassador to the EU, who has expressed his 'great interest [in] what the EU is doing internally . . . on the REFIT programme' (Vincenti 2014).[6]

Concerns about regulatory chill remain

Under pressure as a result of the unexpected civil society contestation of TTIP (see chapter 4), the negotiators, especially on the EU side, have had to promise time and again that no provision in the agreement will lead to a lowering of the level of protection in regulation. We argue that, while this might be true *in a formal* sense – for example, TTIP will most likely not explicitly oblige the EU to lift its ban on hormone-treated beef or force it to scrap its chemicals regulation – the agreement might still affect regulation in a number of *indirect* ways, having a *chilling effect* on current and future levels of protection. We now turn to discuss three reasons as to why the sectoral commitments (relating to specific products and services) and the horizontal disciplines (featuring the 'regulatory cooperation body' described above and applying across the board) foreseen by negotiators give cause for concern despite the many assurances proffered.

We want to warn here against the simplification that the EU *always* has the higher level of protection across the board (see, for example, Wiener et al. 2010). It is generally recognised that, on average over the past decades, the EU[7] has developed higher levels of social and environmental protection than the US (Vogel 2012). For this very reason trade unions in the US are more supportive of TTIP than their European counterparts.[8] But in the area of pharmaceuticals or medical devices, for example, experts and stakeholders (e.g., BEUC 2014b) argue that the regulatory system in the US guarantees at least as high a level of human test subject and patient protection as that in the EU. Another example, and a key bone of contention between the EU and the US in the TTIP negotiations, is the area of financial services. The EU has been pushing to include cooperation on financial regulation in the negotiations, with the US (and in particular its regulators in the Treasury) refusing to do so because of fears that this could undermine the stricter approach to macroprudential regulation established in the US after the financial crisis, nota-bly the Dodd–Frank Act (see Jones and Macartney 2015). Even the USTR's official position of excluding financial regulatory cooperation from the negotiations is insufficient to assuage the fear among some Democratic legislators in Congress, such as Elizabeth Warren (2015), that other elements of the agreement (such as ISDS or market access for financial services providers) could undermine Wall Street reform.[9]

Returning to the issue of regulatory chill, this could, first of all, result from the dynamic effects of mutual recognition if applied in cases where regulations are not completely equivalent in terms of outcomes. Businesses faced with stricter, and hence more costly, regulations may then lobby their governments to move towards the lower-cost standard, threatening relocation to the other party. Negotiators' response to this concern is that sectoral regulatory convergence in TTIP is only about areas where EU and US regulations are different solely *in method* but equivalent *in effect*. To underpin this claim, the same example is usually given, namely that of technical and safety standards for cars (e.g., De

Gucht 2013a).[10] And, even in this case, it has been argued that differences in, for example, the technical standards for bumpers represent different preferences in the EU and the US when it comes to the trade-off between driver protection against car-on-car collisions and pedestrian safety (Asian Trade Centre 2015).

The self-proclaimed ambition of negotiators is to remove not just regulatory differences with regard to car safety but as much as one in two 'actionable' NTBs (in order to realise the ambitious economic gains modelled for TTIP). In the annexes to the study on non-tariff barriers in transatlantic trade discussed in chapter 1 (ECORYS 2009b: 327–52), we find an extensive list of the NTBs identified by experts and industry representatives. It is obvious that this catalogue covers much more than non-sensitive areas about which there might be a relative consensus that EU and US regulations are effectively equivalent. In the list of NTBs we find all those EU regulations that have led to serious friction with the US as well as contributing to Europe's status as a global regulatory leader (see chapter 2): REACH, RoHS, WEEE, the ban on animal testing for cosmetics, the emissions trading scheme in the aviation sector (which has subsequently been watered down) and several directives for energy efficiency. The EU's GMO approval system and its ban on hormone-treated beef are also listed, but – although US industry and influential senators, such as the former Finance Committee Chairman Marc Baucus, 'urge [the USTR] to resolve these and other unwarranted agricultural barriers as part of the FTA negotiations' (US Senate 2013) – we suspect that the USTR realises that directly addressing these is a no-go area. Although there have been previous attempts at regulatory cooperation between the EU and the US in the area of food safety, which saw EU regulators share the view of their US counterparts that there was a need to move towards more 'science-based' risk management, the opposition of Member States and civil society groups (and the presence of multiple veto points within the EU's institutional structure) prevented any successful accommodation (Pollack and Shaffer 2009: 85–112). On the US side, the likes of the Clean Air Act were also singled out by the study as NTBs to be potentially targeted.

For a number of these issues, the negotiators have already had to recognise that achieving meaningful regulatory alignment directly through TTIP is unfeasible.[11] Consider, for example, the wide gap between the respective EU and US regulatory systems for chemicals (REACH and TSCA), which led policymakers to remark at the start of the talks that 'neither full harmonisation nor mutual recognition seems feasible' (European Commission 2013g: 9; see chapter 1). But in other sectors regulatory convergence has to be pursued, otherwise the promises of 'growth and jobs' and 'global regulatory leadership' may fall apart. The key question in all of this is how regulations that fall into the 'grey zone' – between undeniable (and arguably irreconcilable) substantial differences in regulations (such as for food safety and chemicals) and regulations that are obviously different only in their concrete prescriptions but largely equal in effect (such as car headlights) – will be dealt with. Who will decide on their equivalence? On the basis of what criteria? And how far will regulatory alignment go?

A second reason why TTIP might lead to regulatory chill is that, even where joint adoption of international standards rather than mutual recognition (which usually has more of a deregulatory impact) is pursued, this can result in a less ambitious outcome in terms of protection levels than the status quo. An example can be found in the EU's textual proposal for the SPS chapter. This mandates that 'maximum residue levels' (MRLs) of pesticides in food or animal feed adopted within the Codex Alimentarius Commission – a committee of experts which sets internationally recognised food safety standards under the auspices of the UN Food and Agriculture Organisation and World Health Organisation – should be applied between the parties twelve months after their adoption (European Commission 2015b: 3). As the Center for International Environmental Law has shown, 'due to influence of US and corporate lobbying' (Smith et al. 2015: 11ff.), Codex MRLs are in many cases significantly lower than those the EU is applying.

A third (and in our opinion the most important) risk from TTIP can be found in the procedural 'transparency and consultation' disciplines on regulatory policymaking (the 'horizontal' regulatory commitments). According to the EU's proposal, regulatory proposals would have to be sent to the other party for comment by their regulators and stakeholders if requested before being seen by domestic legislatures. NGOs understandably fear that this might slow down regulatory processes and give privileged access to this complex multi-level regulatory system to well-resourced business organisations (see chapter 4). Moreover, the obligation (foreseen by negotiators) to 'take into account' the effect of regulations on transatlantic trade and investment when conducting IAs for new policies might further privilege commercial considerations above others.

When it comes to the horizontal commitments, the key question is what the dynamic effects will be for levels of protection. As EU and US regulations currently often differ (and quite significantly in a number of cases), why should future standards converge smoothly? Will there be a race to the top or a race to the bottom when compared against the current trend? Absent a 'Transatlantic Parliament' – an important difference between the EU's Single Market and the Transatlantic Market envisaged by advocates of TTIP – what will the impact be for democratic decision-making and the legitimacy of future regulations?

These questions are difficult to answer definitively at this stage, but we argue that we can get a better sense of the direction of travel by examining ongoing changes to regulatory politics taking place *within* the EU. We contend that the internal regulatory reform programme not only dovetails with TTIP's underlying philosophy but is also being reinforced by the agreement. For those pushing deregulation in the EU, this is arguably the main objective of the deal.

Cutting red tape from two sides

'Red tape' is being cut vigorously not only through TTIP but also within the EU. Initiated in 2012 under the previous Barroso Commission (but going back to the 2001 Mandelkern Report on Smart Regulation, one of the initiatives coming out of the 2000 Lisbon Agenda), the Regulatory Fitness and Performance Programme (REFIT) is aimed at making EU regulation 'lighter, simpler and less costly'. Alongside TTIP, it is also listed as one of the top priorities of the new Juncker Commission (Juncker

2014). 'Better regulation' is the core area of work of the new First Vice-President of the Commission, Frans Timmermans, who, as Minister of Foreign Affairs of the Netherlands, was involved in a 'subsidiarity review' of EU policies. This is a comparable exercise to the 'Review of the Balance of Competences' being conducted in the UK (Foreign and Commonwealth Office 2012), which may partly explain why Timmermans was welcomed as a choice for the Commission by a British government wrestling with the issue of continued EU membership. Indeed, a first interesting parallel to note between TTIP and the REFIT 'better regulation' project is that both are among the few EU initiatives applauded by the UK government and sometimes explicitly seen as instrumental to keeping the UK in the EU (Traynor and Neslen 2014).[12]

REFIT is the latest initiative in a Commission agenda for 'better' and 'smarter' regulation that is already more than a decade old. In 2007, for example, a target was set to reduce administrative burdens to businesses by 25 per cent by 2012, echoing NTB reduction goals in TTIP. Just as the definition of NTBs has expanded in the area of international trade (with mere differences in regulation between countries being defined as 'red tape'), much the same is true for what accounts for 'red tape' in the case of the EU's internal better and smarter regulation agenda. Where this was originally meant to be focused purely on administrative burdens, it has now come to cover substantial regulations and, according to NGOs and trade unions, to be specifically targeting environmental, health or safety-related (proposals for) regulation. Under REFIT, the European Commission has already decided not to present proposals that it had been preparing on occupational safety and health for hairdressers, musculoskeletal disorders, environmental tobacco smoke, and carcinogens and mutagens. It has also initiated so-called Fitness Checks[13] on regulations for the protection of birds and habitats (called Natura 2000), waste policy and renewable energy (European Commission 2014b).[14]

TTIP and REFIT thus seem driven by very similar interests and to be promoted by a comparable set of ideas. The power of words is being exercised simultaneously on the international and domestic planes. As European Trade Commissioner Cecilia Malmström noted in her confirmation hearing before the European Parliament, 'what can really contribute to growth would be to get rid of the regulatories [sic] and *ease the red tape that is making life difficult for many SMEs in Europe as well*' (2014, emphasis added).[15] This parallel is also reflected in some of the specific criticisms made of the wider 'better regulation' agenda by members of the Stoiber Group. This 'High Level Group on Administrative Burdens', chaired by the former Conservative Minister-President of Bavaria Edmund Stoiber, presented its final report in October 2014.[16] In a dissenting opinion, four members of the group opposed a number of the recommendations in the final report that 'have a clear deregulatory purpose', such as setting a (net) target for reducing regulatory burdens; the obligation to release draft impact assessments for public consultation (which might lead to 'paralysis by analysis'); delaying or obstructing the development of regulations; or strengthening the administrative "competitiveness test" for EU legislation (all very similar to concerns voiced about TTIP). The dissenters argue that 'it is for political decision makers to decide how much *relative* weight to assign to one factor rather than another', again echoing the criticism that TTIP's horizontal disciplines privilege commercial above other considerations in regulatory decision-making (Kosinska et al. 2014: 3). Moreover, it is not just the goal set in the better regulation programme that echoes the (de)regulatory dimension of TTIP, but also the same assurances given to critics that '[REFIT does not] come at the expense of the health and safety of citizens, consumers, workers or of the environment' (European Commission 2014b: 17).

Deregulation as a bargaining chip

One of the objectives of the regulatory cooperation dimension of TTIP is to prevent the occurrence of regulatory differences between the ÈU and the US in the future. The mere fact that *negotiations* are going on may already be having such an effect, leading policymakers to abandon (or tone down) regulatory proposals that may offend the other party. It has been reported that the decision by the European Commission (in February 2013, a few days before the announcement of the TTIP initiative) to drop its ban on beef washed in lactic acid was meant to please the US (*EurActiv* 2013). A link has also been suggested between TTIP and a delay in Commission regulatory proposals to take action against endocrine disrupting chemicals (EDCs) in pesticides (Horel and CEO 2015). The most notorious example of trade negotiations influencing simultaneous domestic regulatory policymaking is the EU's Fuel Quality Directive (FQD), specifically the issue of allocating higher greenhouse gas default values for fuels derived from oil sands and shale oil. These are extracted and refined, respectively, mainly in Canada and the US, and therefore the directive would have the effect of limiting imports from these 'dirtier' sources of oil. Industry in both countries has been lobbying their governments to include the FQD issue in the EU–Canada Comprehensive Economic and Trade Agreement (CETA) and TTIP talks, respectively. Their demands have also been raised by peak business associations such as the Transatlantic Business Council (see Friends of the Earth Europe and Transport and Environment 2014).

These lobbying efforts appear to be having some impact. There have been press reports of the Canadian government threatening to block the CETA negotiations if the EU did not remove tar sands oil from its list of dirty fuels. Meanwhile, USTR Michael Froman has reportedly brought up the FQD during the TTIP negotiations. While in public the USTR states that the US does not want to compromise the EU's substantial climate policy goals and simply has concerns about the lack of transparency and public consultation in the process of writing the FQD, a request by Friends of the Earth Europe for access to documents showed that the US has been lobbying on the substantive issue of the fuel quality standards.[17] Ultimately, the Commission decided not to label tar sands oil as 'dirty' in the FQD. In a statement before the vote on the directive in the European Parliament, BUSINESSEUROPE Director-General Markus J. Beyrer (2014, cited in Crisp 2014) explicitly linked the need for this exemption to broader trade policy imperatives: '[i]n the CETA agreement, the EU and Canada agreed to liberalise trade, including energy . . . By blacklisting oil sand imports from Canada, such a decision would risk imposing trade restrictions on a stable, reliable and democratic country which is a strong economic partner of the EU.'

BUSINESSEUROPE also invoked geopolitical arguments (see

chapter 2) by stating that energy security should be taken into account, as the Ukraine crisis showed the increased need to diversify the EU's energy supply (Crisp 2014). Friends of the Earth Europe and Transport and Environment (2014: 3) have therefore concluded that '[t]rade agreements don't only threaten environmental policy-making upon completion. Environmental regulations currently in the making, such as the FQD, are already being delayed and potentially weakened in the negotiation process.' This concern has even been expressed by more than ten members of the US Congress, who noted that 'trade and investment rules may be being used to undermine or threaten important climate policies of other nations' (Whitehouse et al. 2014).

Giving up policy space through investor protection

The 'chilling effect' of TTIP is also obvious in the proposal to include ISDS in the deal, probably the most contentious issue in the public debate on the negotiations (see chapter 4). Such provisions allow foreign investors to sue governments for perceived violations of their investor rights in independent arbitration tribunals. These usually meet in secret and are composed of three arbitrators, one chosen by either party and a third agreed upon jointly or appointed by one of the organisations managing investor disputes (such as the International Centre for the Settlement of Investment Disputes). Investor rights, as enshrined in numerous bilateral investment treaties (BITs), usually involve provisions not only on 'direct expropriation' – when a government directly takes the property of a foreign investor – but also on 'indirect expropriation' – where a government's regulatory action has an effect 'equivalent' to a direct expropriation, often interpreted by arbitral tribunals to include effects of regulatory decisions on companies' future profit. There is also habitually a requirement for host governments to treat foreign investors 'fairly and equitably', which has frequently been interpreted broadly by arbitrators. In this vein, it has often been remarked in the literature on investment policy that arbitrators not only have considerable leeway in interpreting investment protection but are also far from impartial, insofar as they benefit financially from repeat custom from investors bringing suits against states (Van Harten 2014).

ISDS has been the subject of criticism before, given that an extensive network of BITs with such provisions already exists. But these agreements have mostly been signed between developed and developing countries. In the EU, for example, only a number of Central and Eastern European Member States have such an agreement with the US.[18] The traditional rationale given for BITs is that they are a necessary instrument to supplement under-developed legal systems and 'depoliticise' investment disputes between states that might otherwise 'turn ugly' (the image of the 'gunboat diplomacy' of the nineteenth century between colonial powers and the 'colonised' is often invoked; for example, Puig 2013: 601). In the context of a trade and investment agreement between two economies with largely developed legal systems, where disputes involving investors are not known to escalate into major cross-cutting political conflicts, such justifications do ring a little hollow. Rather, such tribunals 'provide significant advantages to multinational enterprises at the expense of governmental flexibility' by establishing a system of privatised transnational governance (Van Harten 2005: 600). Although they cannot formally strike down laws, the damages they award may ultimately result in regulatory chill, much like TTIP's proposed provisions on regulatory cooperation (Poulsen et al. 2015).

Ultimately, ISDS is consistent with the broader depoliticisation of regulatory politics being pushed for in the agreement. This does not quite amount to the 'horror story' of some critics of TTIP that ISDS amounts to a 'full-frontal assault on democracy' orchestrated by corporations (Monbiot 2013; see also Wallach 2012). In general, the evidence suggests that foreign investors (read multinationals) are often not clamouring for investor protection provisions (e.g., Basedow 2014) – although it must be said that they have pushed for such provisions to be included in TTIP (see, for example, BUSINESSEUROPE 2014: 9). As noted above, legal systems in the EU and the US are well developed, and thus suits are less likely, while tribunals cannot strike down laws (they can only award damages). Finally, the European Commission was, at the time of writing, proposing a series of reforms to ISDS, such as increased transparency, a roster for arbitrators, and a greater 'carve out' from investor protection provisions for regulatory measures, which may render 'abuse' of the system by multinationals less probable (see chapter 4). That said, the conclusion reached by a number of experts in the field is that ISDS in TTIP 'may impose non-trivial costs, in the form of litigation expenses and *reduced policy space*'. Moreover 'an investment chapter *would almost certainly give foreign investors greater rights than they currently enjoy under EU and member state law*' (Poulsen et al. 2015: 1, emphasis added). Its effects may thus be more subtle than the furore around the provision suggests, but still important.

Taking the politics out of regulation?

TTIP is aimed mainly at eliminating regulatory differences between the EU and the US. Such differences, which get in the way of achieving the theoretical construct of a global free market, have over the past decades been reframed as 'red tape' - both within the international trading system and domestically (as the EU's REFIT agenda highlights). For one, TTIP is pursuing the elimination of regulatory differences directly through commitments in specific sectors, with mutual recognition as the preferred approach. But negotiators are also conscious of the political and administrative limits to achieving mutual recognition through TTIP. They are therefore pursuing 'horizontal' cooperation, establishing rules and institutions that should help bring about future regulatory convergence and discipline domestic regulatory policymaking. We have warned of the risk that this might lead to regulatory chill.

These effects can be expected from TTIP even if we accept negotiators' promise that no commitments in the agreement will formally lower existing levels of protection. They discipline market-correcting policies and tilt the state–market balance further towards the latter. Bronwen Morgan (2003) has critically reviewed such reforms of the *process* of regulation, also known as 'meta-regulation'.[19] She calls the social logic behind this meta-regulation an example of 'nonjudicial legality' leading to the 'economisation' of regulatory politics. Regulatory policy choices become expressed increasingly in terms of 'market failures' or 'distortions' instead of need, vulnerability or harm. The result, and arguably the aim, of this process is the silencing of alternative modes of justice, especially those relying on moral or distributive justice – as the case of ISDS and the privileging of investor rights starkly illustrates.

This chapter has highlighted the redefinition of regulation in economistic 'cost' terms at the level both of the global trading system and of domestic regulatory processes, which is being rein-forced by TTIP. Regulators tend to internalise the administrative disciplines that oblige them strictly to prove that their proposals hinder the free market – and transatlantic trade in particular – as little as possible, and are thus likely to be increasingly socialised within the 'trade environment' in which they are compelled to cooperate with their counterparts across the Atlantic. Moreover, while it might sound reassuring that regulators are actively involved in the TTIP talks (and other trade agreement negotia-tions), they are playing an 'away game' against trade negotiators who are on home turf when it comes to negotiating such deals. It was often recognised during our interviews with trade nego-tiators[20] that there are often deep divides between their 'trade perspective' and the perspective of regulators.

This 'economisation of regulatory politics' – and in particular ISDS – has, however, been hotly contested by NGOs, leading us straight into the next chapter. Here we elaborate on how the attempt to take the politics out of regulatory policy in TTIP might actually end up by (re)introducing the politics into trade policy.

4

Challenging TTIP

Having outlined some of the specific issues in the TTIP negotiations, we take a step back to reflect on what these say about the wider state of global trade politics. The agreement is arguably the most controversial trade deal in over a decade. In Britain, George Monbiot (2013) has been one of the most high-profile personalities to write of the 'threat' posed by TTIP to 'democracy' and the 'rule of law'. In the US, groups formed to campaign against NAFTA in the 1990s, such as Public Citizen's Global Trade Watch, have warned of TTIP as a Trojan horse, surreptitiously bringing about (in the words of founder Lori Wallach) the 'dismantling of all social, consumer and environmental protection' (Wallach 2013).

Despite such statements, much of the opposition to the agreement from civil society groupings (and some political parties) has been concentrated in Europe, where a 'Stop TTIP' campaign has taken off (US groups have been focusing most of their attentions on TPP). One of its achievements has been a European Citizens' Initiative (ECI) (a pan-EU petition) against TTIP that has garnered over 1.8 million signatures (and counting). A highly technical Commission consultation on the proposed ISDS mechanism saw over 100,000 submissions. And the Twitter hashtags #StopTTIP, #noTTIP and just simply #TTIP are alive with the mostly critical chatter of NGOs, activists and ordinary citizens.

Aside from involving many of the same groups and activists, a number of the arguments in the Stop/No TTIP campaign mirror those of the anti-globalisation protests of the late 1990s and early 2000s – famous for the 1999 'Battle in Seattle' at the intended launch of the 'Millennium Round'. The specifics of the debate, of course, are somewhat different today, but it is very interesting to see how many of the problems identified back then – especially the fear that trade and investment agreements undermine democratic legitimacy and strengthen the hands of multinational corporations – are once again on the political agenda. Such criticisms have also been emphasised in much of the critical, Marxist-inspired literature, which points to the power of transnational capital elites in 'constitutionalising' (or legally enshrining) neoliberal globalisation via trade agreements (Gill 1995; Raza 2014).

In this chapter we show that TTIP is not turning into a story of unchecked corporate power. No longer trapped within the confines of technocratic decision-making, trade policy has become (re)politicised. We set the scene by providing a brief overview of the changing nature of societal mobilisation on global trade politics. As international trade negotiations have increasingly centred on 'behind-the-border' trade measures, there has been a shift away from purely *distributive* trade conflict (involving competing economic interests) to conflicts centred on civil society groups' *normative* critique of the expansion of the international trade agenda, in particular the anti-globalisation protests at the turn of the century. The success of these 'transnational advocacy networks' (Keck and Sikkink 1998) lay in their ability to reframe discursively the global trade and investment regime as a threat to fundamental values.

This is a similar dynamic to the one we are seeing in the case of the campaign against TTIP being conducted predominantly by European civil society groups, which are our focus in this chapter. The increasing furore around the transatlantic negotiations points to the difficulties of selling free trade using economistic arguments (such as economic modelling; see chapter 1) or the idea that the agreement will 'set global standards' (see chapter 2), both of which business groups and allied policymakers have sought to do. So far, and illustrating the EU locus of the civil society campaign, it has prompted the European Commission to suspend negotiations on the ISDS mechanism, tone down some of its proposals on regulatory convergence, and release more trade negotiating documents than ever before in a transparency drive. Thus, while the initiation of TTIP and the agenda of regulatory depoliticisation behind it represent an important instance of corporate influence, its negotiation has shown that the public sphere holds considerable room for contestation from civil society and limits the oft-remarked structural power of business (Sell and Prakash 2004: 169). TTIP is thus a potential 'game-changer' in global trade politics, but in a different way than its initiators intended.

Changing patterns of mobilisation

Before we turn to these issues, it is important to understand what animated trade politics during much of the postwar, 'embedded liberal' period we discussed in the previous chapter. The purpose of the global economic institutions set up in the postwar period – the International Monetary Fund, (what is now known as) the World Bank and the GATT – was to ensure that global trade and economic governance more broadly was put on an ordered footing. The GATT, more specifically, was supposed to provide a framework in which trade liberalisation could take place 'with a view to raising standards of living', as its preamble made clear.

There was also an 'embedded' side to the liberal postwar settlement. The term itself is from Karl Polanyi's seminal work *The Great Transformation* (1944), in which he wrote of the destructiveness of unbridled, free market capitalism in the lead up to the Second World War. It had become, in his words, 'disembedded' from society, causing huge socioeconomic dislocation that culminated in the rise of extremist parties and the breakdown of international order. *Re-embedding* capitalism became, according to John Gerrard Ruggie, the objective of the architects of the postwar system of global economic governance, 'a framework which would safeguard and even aid the quest for domestic stability without, at the same time, triggering the mutually destructive external consequences that had plagued the interwar period' (Ruggie 1982: 393). Preserving domestic policy space was seen as key as a means of enabling the more interventionist policies of emerging welfare states that had been seen as lacking in the aftermath of the Great Depression. As a result, the 1947 GATT included a whole host of 'safeguards, exemptions, exceptions, and restrictions . . . to protect a variety of domestic social policies' (ibid.: 396).

This postwar system of global trade governance was characterised predominantly by distributive trade conflict. Trade politics was about who gained from opening markets and who lost – and how these gains and losses were spread out among various groups. As Dani Rodrik (2011: 57) has pointed out for the US economy, every dollar of income generated from trade liberalisation implies shifting around $50 in the economy. If we examine the set-up of traditional trade theory, this is completely focused on explaining the conflict between those with an interest in protectionism and those with an interest in liberalisation. Crucially, the GATT, with its emphasis on reciprocal trade negotiations, was set up so that 'governments relied mainly on the mobilization of export-oriented business lobbies to counter domestic protectionist opposition' by pushing for sustained multilateral market-opening, in what became known as the 'bicycle theory' (Walter 2001: 54). You had to keep 'pedalling' (liberalising) to keep the 'bicycle' (trading system) from falling over.

While mobilising exporters became one element of the depoliticising rationale of 'embedded liberalism', the other was the consensus that domestic policy space had to be preserved to allow states to pursue interventionist macroeconomic policies. Welfare states played a role in mitigating the effects of trade liberalisation, taking (at least some of) the redistributive sting out of the liberal trade regime (Rodrik 2011). The liberalisation undertaken in the first few decades of GATT negotiations thus focused on 'at the border' measures.

It was not until the Uruguay Round (1986–94) that the content of trade negotiations substantially changed. While tariffs remained on the agenda, the 'new trade politics' brought trade into the realm of domestic regulation, as we have discussed in previous chapters. Combined with subsequent bilateral trade agreements covering similar issues, they are generally acknowledged to have eaten into the policy space of (especially developing) countries, effectively constraining their ability to pursue effective industrial policy (Wade 2003). Moreover, these rules could now be enforced via an effective and independent dispute settlement mechanism – in contrast to the GATT, where a dispute panel's ruling could be blocked by the objection of a single member, rendering the system unenforceable.

This growing intrusiveness of the global trade and investment regime was increasingly contested by what could be called the 'new kids on the (trade politics) block' – (transnational) civil society actors, often referred to as NGOs.[1] Protests against the GATT's 1991 tuna–dolphin ruling – which had found against US policy banning exports of tuna that did not meet certain dolphin-protection standards – and NAFTA were early instances of such activism. But the protests against the Multilateral Agreement on Investment (MAI) proved to be a watershed moment, with its eventual failure seen as key in 'stimulating the rise of an anti-capitalist movement that has increasingly challenged the operation of multilateral economic institutions' (Egan 2001: 91). Activists framed the proposed agreement – which would have strengthened the rights of foreign investors and given them access to an ISDS mechanism – as a 'corporate rule treaty' that threatened national and popular sovereignty (cited in Johnston and Laxer 2003: 53), contributing to the indefinite suspension of the OECD negotiations on the MAI in 1998 (Walter 2001; Johnston and Laxer 2003). Many of the same organisations would later also participate in the emblematic 'Battle in Seattle' protests at the 1999 WTO Ministerial; the campaign against the GATS 2000 negotiations aiming to expand the scope of the GATS and the activism around the launch of the Doha Round (Gill 2000; Strange 2011). A new communications tool, the internet, facilitated the transmission of information and thus the emergence of these global networks of activists, even if some saw these merely as 'tools' for internal communication that were not instrumental in defeating such agreements as the MAI (Warkentin and Mingst 2000; Johnston and Laxer 2003: 62).

While some see this mobilisation of civil society groups – often referred to as the 'anti/alter-globalisation movement' – as a cohesive, global social movement or evidence of the emergence of 'global civil society', many others have preferred to use the looser term of 'transnational advocacy network' (Johnston and Laxer 2003: 47-9). This comes from the work of Keck and Sikkink (1998: 1), who define such groups as 'networks of activists, distinguishable largely by the centrality of principled ideas or values in motivating their formation'. Rather than seeking a mass mobilisation of citizens, as in 'transnational social movements', what such networks (composed of a smaller number of dedicated activists, or issue/norm 'entrepreneurs') have primarily centred on is changing the terms of debate, (re)framing issues discursively in the public sphere to put pressure on political leaders. Such campaigns have also often been limited by their issue-specific nature, which has constricted the capacity for long-term campaigning (Morin 2011).

While we return to this issue in more depth below, at this point it is worth briefly reflecting on the impact these transnational activists had on the nature of trade politics. The mobilisation of NGOs at Seattle and other trade meetings, and their notable successes (e.g., contributing to failure of the MAI or the Doha Declaration on TRIPs), suggests that trade policy was no longer just about economic interests fighting it out for the spoils of trade liberalisation. Rather, it featured 'principled' – to use Keck and Sikkink's term – opposition to the global trade (and investment) regime and its wider impact on society. Trade politics, in a sense, has become about the 'everyday', impacting the way in which citizens lead their daily lives (Hobson and Seabrooke 2007). In the manner of a few other scholars, who have similarly focused on the 'everyday' politics of global trade (e.g., Hurt et al. 2013), we refer to this as 'normative' trade conflict. NGOs helped to change the terms of debates in global trade policy, centring it on value-based questions that pertain to everyone's daily lives (e.g., democracy, food safety standards, public services). Where the 'embedded liberalism' of the postwar trade regime had married domestic policy autonomy and a general commitment to trade liberalisation, limiting conflicts over trade to distributive questions resulting from the removal of tariffs, the new regime threatened to 'disembed' markets by constraining public policy in the interest of liberalisation, allegedly entrenching the power of big business. This is not of course to say that distributive trade conflict had disappeared – as the involvement of trade unions concerned with 'outsourcing' attests to – but rather that new debates had taken centre stage (at least for the time being).

Of course, not all organisations rejected the global trade regime wholesale. It is important to distinguish between those 'rejectionists' who objected to globalised capitalism *per se* and those 'reformist' organisations that wanted to work within the system to improve the structures of global economic governance (the terminology is from Scholte 2003). What is more, there is evidence to suggest that NGOs active on trade issues have sought increasingly to position themselves as 'reformists' in order to gain credibility among trade policymakers at the WTO. Critical, high-profile public campaigns have in many cases turned to routinised technical work and the provision of expertise (e.g., to understaffed developing country WTO missions) (Hopewell 2009; Hannah 2014). Combined with the stagnation of the Doha Round of global trade talks, this may also have contributed to explaining why some of the NGO activists we interviewed noted a slowdown in global activism on trade issues from the mid-2000s onwards.[2] Although a number of other trade issues have prompted spirited NGO campaigns since then – most notably the Economic Partnership Agreements being negotiated between the EU and the African, Caribbean and Pacific states and the Anti-Counterfeiting Trade Agreement (ACTA) – the emergence of TTIP (and its level of 'disembedding' ambition) is seen by several of these activists as a new defining moment in the history of civil society activism on trade issues.[3]

NGOs and the TTIP negotiations

Civil society groups in the US, while also speaking out on the issue of a transatlantic trade deal, have thus far focused their energies largely on the TPP negotiations between the US and Pacific

Rim states. This is not entirely surprising if we consider that these negotiations are in a much more advanced stage and also appear to be the priority of the Obama administration (Lauer and Ducourtieux 2015). TTIP, moreover, is seen by some civil society groups as a means of harmonising US standards upwards towards those in Europe in a number of areas, notably by the US trade union movement (AFL-CIO 2015), while the TPP's effects are more broadly perceived as deregulatory and imperilling US jobs.

As a result, it is NGOs in Europe which have led what has been a crescendo of voices opposed to the agreement (either in its entirety or particular aspects thereof). The starting gun for this activism was the approval of the EU negotiating mandate for TTIP and the start of talks in June and July 2013. The lead was originally taken by a series of NGOs with a history of campaigning on trade issues in Brussels, the so-called Seattle-to-Brussels Network (S2B), whose most prominent members were Corporate Europe Observatory (CEO), the Transnational Institute (TNI) and various members of the Association for the Taxation of Financial Transactions and Aid to Citizens (ATTAC) network, all veterans of the first major mobilisation against trade and investment agreements of the late 1990s and early 2000s.[4] That is not to say that the campaign against TTIP simply 'came out of nowhere' in 2013. As one prominent NGO activist involved in S2B's work informed us, much of the preparatory work of the campaign had been done in the years before, where the network had focused on studying and highlighting the implications of the EU's new competence for negotiating on investment in a series of policy papers (e.g., S2B 2010).[5]

Partly as a result, much of the early criticism of the trade deal (from the summer to late 2013), and in particular by CEO, which took a leading role in the emerging public debate on TTIP, focused on ISDS (CEO 2013a, 2013b; S2B 2013). This first phase of the campaign culminated in a letter to De Gucht in December 2013, signed by almost 200 NGOs (mostly European, but also including some US organisations), voicing their 'opposition to the inclusion of [ISDS] in [TTIP]' (CEO et al. 2013: 1). In response to 'unprecedented public interest in the talks', the Commission announced soon after (in January 2014) that it was suspending negotiations on the issue, pending the outcome of a public consultation (European Commission 2014a). It also established a TTIP Advisory Group featuring 'experts' from both business and civil society to 'provide EU trade negotiators with high quality advice in the areas being negotiated' (European Commission 2014e).

Of course, ISDS was not the only issue to feature in the campaign against the agreement (even at this early stage). November 2013 saw the launch of the Alternative Trade Mandate, a series of preliminary and wide-ranging ideas on 'alternatives to the current trade and investment regime', including greater respect for social and environmental objectives beyond trade and a 'fair[er] distribution of income within global value chains' (Alternative Trade Mandate 2013: 2–5). The 'chlorinated chicken' became a symbol strongly associated with the negotiations in a number of EU Member States (notably Germany), while complaints about hormone-treated beef also made the rounds (Faoila 2014). Throughout, NGOs have also vociferously bemoaned the lack of transparency in the negotiations and the supposedly privileged access given to business lobbyists. But it is certainly fair to say that ISDS has been a key lightning rod of opposition: the public consultation held on the issue between March and July 2014, and which was based on a somewhat arcane and legalistic document (European Commission 2014f), attracted a total of 149,399 responses from across the EU (European Commission 2015d), even if most responses were templates submitted at the instance of civil society campaigns in a number of Member States. This unexpectedly high level of interest crashed the website, and the Commission was forced to extend the deadline by ten days (European Commission 2014g).

At least partly in response to this activism, Member States that had previously unanimously supported the inclusion of ISDS in the EU's negotiating mandate appeared to be getting cold feet (*EurActiv* 2015a). The normally quite pro-liberalisation Germany[6] first adopted a notably critical line in March 2014 on the inclusion of ISDS in TTIP (Donnan and Wagstyl 2014), a position also subsequently echoed by other Member States (such as France) and several national parliaments (including Austria's National Assembly, the Dutch Lower House and the French Senate). The elections for the European Parliament (held in May 2014) also saw various European political parties take an often critical stance on TTIP, especially regarding ISDS. Both the European Greens and the Left Group oppose TTIP and investor arbitration. The Social Democratic group, in turn, has so far taken a more hedged position of conditional support for a transatlantic trade deal provided this does not lower standards. They have, however, also called for the removal of ISDS – even if they appear to be more divided on the issue. For its part, while the conservative European People's Party has generally taken a more 'pro-TTIP' line, its candidate for the Commission presidency (Jean-Claude

Juncker) was forced to concede during the European election campaign that a 'lowering of standards' was not 'negotiable' (cited in De Ville and Siles-Brügge 2014a). Events[7] surrounding the nomination hearing of the new Trade Commissioner Cecilia Malmström (in September 2014) suggested that the Commission President was far less keen on ISDS than the former (De Gruyter 2014), with Juncker ultimately delegating responsibility for deciding on the final inclusion of ISDS to Commission Vice-President Frans Timmermans (*Financial Times* 2014). Equally illustrative of the increasing toxicity of the issue is the furore surrounding the previously uncontroversial EU–Canada CETA agreement. NGOs had been warning that CETA might become a 'Trojan horse' for TTIP, with US subsidiaries in Canada making use of its provisions on investor arbitration (Eberhardt et al. 2014). In this increasingly hostile climate, Germany made a number of critical statements on CETA's ISDS provisions, delaying signature of the agreement, originally scheduled for September 2014 (Hall 2014; *EurActiv* 2014a).[8]

Meanwhile another major initiative took off. First proposed by a coalition of German NGOs, and involving a number of veterans of the NGO campaigns on trade in the 1990s/early 2000s, an ECI opposed to TTIP and CETA was launched in July 2014. ECIs are an instrument under EU law that allow EU citizens to call directly on the Commission to propose a legal act in an area of EU competence provided they obtain 1 million signatures (including minimum signature thresholds in at least seven EU Member States). Despite garnering a considerable number of signatures in a short period of time over the summer, the ECI was originally rejected by the Commission in September 2014 on the technical grounds that calling for the repeal of a negotiation mandate did 'not fall within the scope of the Regulation' on ECIs (European Commission 2014h: 2). Notwithstanding this setback, the organisers decided to continue their campaign of collecting signatures, rebranding the ECI as a 'self-organised European Citizens' Initiative' (sECI) and taking the Commission to the European Court of Justice (Stop TTIP 2015a). The sECI reached a million signatures on 4 December 2014 and, as of May 2015, had collected over 1.8 million signatures and met the Member State threshold (Stop TTIP 2015b) – one of only a very small number of ECIs to do so.

All this campaigning from NGOs has had a direct effect on the approach taken by the Commission to the negotiations, and not just on ISDS. As we saw in chapter 3, it was forced to tone down its initial proposals (from 2013) for the scope of the horizontal regulatory cooperation chapter so that (in documents released in January 2015) the regulatory cooperation body to be created would 'not have the power to adopt legal acts'. Moreover, the arrival of the new Trade Commissioner, Cecilia Malmström – who is generally considered to be a more effective communicator than her predecessor, Karel De Gucht – coincided with the announcement of a 'fresh start' to the negotiations (European Commission 2014i; European Commission 2015e). This involved, most significantly, a 'transparency initiative', which complemented measures aimed at engaging with critics put in place by her predecessor De Gucht: the TTIP Advisory Group; a relatively active twitter feed (@EU_TTIP_Team) and the official declassification of the EU's negotiating mandate by the Council of Ministers, although a leaked version of this document had already been available for over a year. Malmström's initiative saw the Commission change the confidentiality rules for the access to documents by Members of the European Parliament (MEP) (allowing all MEPs, rather than just some on the International Trade Committee [INTA] to access negotiating texts) and, most importantly, publishing numerous negotiating texts tabled by the EU. This, it should be stressed, is an unprecedented level of openness for EU trade negotiations as, previously, access to such documents was routinely rebuffed on the grounds that this might 'undermine the protection of the public interest as regards international relations' (Regulation [EC] No 1049/2001) – to which our experience as researchers in this area can attest. In January 2015 the Commission also released its report on the ISDS consultation, which acknowledged the widespread opposition to the provision and suggested a number of areas for improvements to the system of investor arbitration (European Commission 2015d). Emboldened by the transparency initiative and ISDS report, NGOs have continued to exert considerable pressure on these two issues – 'fresh start' notwithstanding. Much was made of the ISDS report finding that 97 per cent of the (mostly duplicate) responses to the consultation rejected the inclusion of the provision (with many also expressing scepticism about TTIP in general; see, for example, CEO 2015). In our interviews, civil society groups also suggested to us that they had seized upon Malmström's new emphasis on transparency in order to push for the publication of consolidated, negotiating texts (which were still secret) and 'institutionalise' transparency for the future.[9]

A transnational movement?

'As I get my placard ready for tomorrow's protest, it really starts to dawn on me, that this is not just a TTIP campaign – this is the start of a movement' (Sheikh 2015). Penned in February 2015, these are the reflections of one UK activist. But can we really speak of a cohesive 'transnational social movement' against TTIP? Or are we seeing the workings of what would best be characterised as a transnational advocacy network?

As during the anti-globalisation protests of the 1990s, there has been extensive use of the internet in the anti-TTIP campaign. Much of the activism has been channelled through mailing lists, social media platforms such as Twitter, and the blogosphere. The ECI/sECI have been circulated via the internet, while the response to the ISDS consultation owes much to 'internet-based' NGOs or 'dotcauses' (Clark and Themudo 2006) such as 38 Degrees in the UK or Campact in Germany. There has, however, been no mass mobilisation of the public. Indeed, there is some evidence to suggest that anti-TTIP groups are overrepresented on social media platforms (Bauer 2015). Opinion polls suggest that most Europeans (58 per cent) and Americans (53 per cent) are in favour of a trade and investment agreement between the EU and US, with only the public in Germany, Austria and Luxembourg being mostly against a possible TTIP (European Commission 2014j: 32; Pew Research Centre 2014). While there have been several public demonstrations against TTIP, the most significant of these to date, a Europe-wide protest on 11 October 2014 and a similar 'global day of action' against free trade agreements (including TTIP and TPP) on 18 April 2015, resulted in somewhat limited turnout. For example, in Germany (which has one of the most heated national debates on TTIP), the better attended 'global day of action' attracted protestors only in the low tens of thousands nationwide (*EurActiv* 2014b; *Der Spiegel* 2015).

Moreover, this activism is concentrated on the European side of the Atlantic. US organisations such as Public Citizen (and specifically its Global Trade Watch division) have campaigned on the issue – explicitly seeking to link TTIP to the controversial NAFTA by referring to it as TAFTA (Public Citizen 2015) – and have collaborated with their European counterparts on formulating joint positions and coordinating their campaigns. However, in the US, TTIP has attracted far less attention than the TPP in the controversial debate over US fast-track authority. Even within Europe, and despite considerable activism from Brussels-based NGOs that was confirmed in our interviews with NGO representatives and Commission officials,[10] the response in individual countries has varied considerably. If we examine the ISDS consultation, the UK, Austria and Germany together accounted for 79 per cent of the submissions (European Commission 2015d), while many others, including somewhat sizeable countries (e.g., Poland, Italy), had fewer than 300 submissions each. There is a similar variation in the number of signatures of the ECI/sECI (Stop TTIP 2015b). Thus, we have the anomaly of countries such as the UK and Germany, where TTIP has been the subject of parliamentary debates, regular news programmes and demonstrations, and which possess relatively well-organised anti-TTIP NGO coalitions, and others where the issue has barely been discussed at all in the public sphere.

Yet despite the fact that the campaign appears to be limited to the work of specific organisations (which we could refer to as 'issue entrepreneurs') working in a (sometimes fragmented) transnational advocacy network, it has still managed to put advocates of TTIP on the defensive and impacted on the actual content of the negotiations, telling a story of circumscribed corporate power. What is more, the level of ambition present in TTIP has allowed campaigners, in many ways, to cut across the issue-specific nature of previous campaigns on trade and investment issues (consider, for example, the focus in the MAI campaign on 'corporate rule' or on public services in the case of the GATS).

The difficulties in selling free trade

'Insofar as a public debate on TTIP exists, EU Member States are losing it. In part this is because they are engaging in it fitfully and invariably on the back foot' (House of Lords 2014: 72). Thus notes a UK House of Lords report on TTIP from May 2014. Since then, the Commission has also been forced to admit that 'credibility and trust are still at low level[s]' (Council of the EU 2014a: 6). This is especially problematic from a policymaker perspective if we consider that the European Parliament will have to give its assent to any trade deal. This may well also apply to national parliaments if the agreement is considered to be of 'shared' or 'mixed' Member State and EU competence. As a result, 'selling' TTIP to a sceptical audience is one of the priorities for the new Trade Commissioner Cecilia Malmström, as spelled out clearly in Commission President Jean-Claude Juncker's mission letter for the Trade portfolio (European Commission 2014l: 4). It has also featured as an issue in several conclusions of EU Member State bodies such as the Foreign Affairs Council and the European Council (Council of the EU 2014b; *EurActiv* 2015b).

Meanwhile, the debate in the US over renewing TPA has also been marked by the vociferous opposition from trade unions and other civil society groupings, although most of the focus of the administration and civil society groups has been on TPP rather than TTIP (see Hamilton 2014: 87). Barack Obama will have to rely on support from the Republican Party in order to pass TPA, after the opposition of the then Democratic Senate Majority Leader, Harry Reid, prevented the president from obtaining fast-track authority in 2014 (Mauldin and Hughes 2014; Donnan 2015).

Moreover, we have already seen how the anti-TTIP campaign has shaped the approach to the negotiations on the EU side, with negotiations on ISDS being suspended, proposals on regulatory cooperation being toned down and a new 'transparency initiative' being inaugurated. From the perspective of negotiators and business interests, this was not how things were meant to be. On the EU side, in particular, the Commission had its eye on the need for a PR strategy to counter the NGO narrative, focused on selling the economic gains to be realised from TTIP (enter the econometric modelling we discussed in chapter 1) and emphasising its contribution to Europe's global standing (see chapter 2). The USTR had also been touting the 'growth and jobs' potential of TTIP and its contribution to global rule-setting.

Selling trade liberalisation

Both EU and US policymakers and pro-free trade business interests have a history of using the first type of economistic argument, in particular, to depoliticise trade policymaking and push for trade liberalisation.[11] More recently, drawing on such ideas has allowed the EU to pursue a fairly activist trade policy despite the pressures induced by the crisis. The message has been that Europe has no choice but to keep markets open, as trade with third parties offers a means of offsetting flagging EU demand. Thus, despite the vociferous opposition of the European car industry, the year 2011 saw the EU sign its most ambitious FTA yet with South Korea, because policymakers were able to paint the agreement as a 'necessity' given the importance of boosting EU competitiveness in a globalised economy. This isolated the car sector, widely seen as 'a protectionist hangover that had failed to adapt to the changing nature of the global economy' (Siles-Brügge 2014: 120). What this suggests is the success of such narratives in dealing with the classic, distributive sources of trade conflict – between those businesses standing to gain materially from trade opening and those standing to lose out. Painting the losers as 'protectionist' special interests, getting in the way of the increased welfare for everyone resulting from trade liberalisation (as argued *ad infinitum* by mainstream economists), has long served to stigmatise opponents of trade agreements. The word 'protectionist' is one of the worst insults in mainstream economists' vocabulary – with this policy prescription widely (and erroneously) seen in trade policy circles as a major *cause* and *contributor* to the Great Depression when it actually was more of a *symptom* (Strange 1985).

The case of TTIP illustrates the limitations of discursively *depoliticising* the agreement. This is because the agreement is less an instance of *distributive* trade conflict and more one of *normative* trade conflict, with the battle lines drawn largely between business interests, which are overwhelmingly in favour (see chapter 3), and civil society organisations – rather than between different economic interests (as in traditional political economy theory). While normative conflict is hardly new (as noted by our discussion of the establishment of the WTO), TTIP goes beyond the WTO in terms of its 'disembedding' ambitions and impact on the 'everyday', featuring two of the countries having taken the lead in pushing for greater 'behind-the-border' liberalisation at the WTO and in bilateral trade deals. As a result, TTIP plainly illustrates how there are clear limits to the 'economisation of regulatory politics' we saw in chapter 3 – that is, the attempt to depoliticise socioeconomic regulation by depicting it in strictly economic terms, as a non-tariff *barrier* to trade – which has been a central objective of the agenda of trade negotiators in TTIP.

The depth of normative conflict surrounding TTIP is illustrated in part by examining the types of organisations that have mobilised. It has not just elicited criticism from the 'usual suspects' – 'rejectionist' NGOs – but has also involved others adopting a more 'reformist' position. One of the most prominent organisations campaigning on the agreement, BEUC – the pan-European organisation representing consumers (see chapter 3) and a member of the TTIP Advisory Group – explicitly states on its website that '[a] free trade agreement could benefit consumers' (BEUC 2015). Similarly, the official position of the principal labour organisations, the European Trade Union Confederation (ETUC) and the AFL-CIO, is not one of outright rejection: although concerned about the agreement's potential impact on workers, they have stated that this 'can help create quality job growth with shared prosperity on both sides of the Atlantic if the project is approached and concluded in an open, democratic and participatory fashion' (ETUC and AFL-CIO 2014: 1). A number of NGO representatives stressed to us that there is a concerted attempt to approach the Commission with 'constructive proposals', as this lends greater legitimacy to their concerns.[12] But, in the case of TTIP, we argue that this hardly amounts to the routinised accommodation and mere provision of technical expertise that has characterised much recent NGO involvement at the WTO (see, for example, Hannah 2014). Despite not opposing the negotiations outright, BEUC, ETUC and the AFL-CIO have made their support conditional on TTIP not adversely affecting existing levels of social, environmental and consumer protection in the EU and the US. In this vein, they have contributed to an important critical narrative on TTIP emerging thanks to NGO activism.

TTIP according to NGOs

One of the lightning rods for the opposition has been the trade agreement's proposed investor protection provisions, and more specifically ISDS. While there have been some nuances in the ISDS debate, a position common to most NGOs has been one of outright opposition to its inclusion in TTIP. This is because of the perception that it unduly favours foreign investors over governments' ability to regulate in the public interest. The very idea that the rights of *foreign* investors need additional protection is seen – at the more 'rejectionist' end of the NGO spectrum – as an example of a 'transatlantic corporate bill of rights' (CEO 2013a), while more 'reformist' groups have emphasised its 'discriminatory' nature, as it can be accessed only by foreign firms. Crucially, a fear consistently expressed by groups critical of ISDS is that 'consumer, health, labour and environmental regulations are regularly challenged as violations of "investor rights"' (BEUC 2014c: 1). More specifically, the ability of arbitration tribunals to find against governments and impose costly awards is seen to threaten the regulatory capacity of states. NGOs have consistently referred to the 'regulatory chill effect' that ISDS may impose on governments, who – fearing costly arbitration suits – will avoid legislating in the first place (CEO 2014a).[13] Turning to the functioning of the arbitration system itself, the concern is that this is unduly skewed towards the rights of investors: not only are proceedings held in secret, but there is a systemic conflict of interest in a system that relies on repeat custom from foreign investors, who are the only ones who can bring claims. A final line of criticism that is sometimes heard is that the system itself is unnecessary to protect foreign investors, as the judiciaries of EU Member States and the US already adequately protect their interests (CEO et al. 2013: 2). In sum, while there is some variation in the positions of various groups, ISDS is fairly consistently rejected on the principled grounds that, in the words of the December 2013 letter opposing ISDS signed by over 200 NGOs, it 'undermines democratic decision-making' (ibid.).

While ISDS has taken up much of the NGOs' time, the issue of regulatory convergence has also featured quite prominently in the campaigns of most, from rejectionists such as CEO to reformists such as BEUC and ETUC. There is a fear that TTIP will lead to a watering down of legitimate regulations in the interest of cutting 'red tape' for business. We have already dedicated much space to this in chapter 3, so we will recapitulate these arguments only briefly here. Firstly, there is a fear that TTIP will lead to a 'race to the bottom' in standards across the Atlantic, and especially (although not exclusively) in Europe, which tends to have higher levels of risk regulation. As a result, chlorinated chickens and American hormone-treated beef, the dangers of indiscriminately importing the US practice of 'fracking' for gas, and the risk of lowering labour rights have become clarion calls on the EU side for much of the campaigning on TTIP (Faoila 2014; Friends of the Earth Europe 2014b; ETUC 2013). Secondly, there is the fear that, as a result of its provisions on regulatory cooperation, TTIP could become a 'living agreement' that has a 'chilling effect' (much like ISDS) on future regulation. According to a report prepared by CEO, this would mean that 'future decision-making [on regulating socioeconomic risks] will go underground, escape democratic scrutiny and be wide open to business lobbying' (CEO 2013c). In a similar vein, NGOs have begun to draw links between TTIP and the EU's wider REFIT programme, with the concern being that the negotiations with the US are being used as an excuse to strike down regulations in the EU, most notably the FQD and the regulation of EDCs (see chapter 3).

Finally, and as the discussions over the 'living agreement' have shown, a key issue for NGOs has been transparency and the broader process of trade negotiations, particularly on the European side. A persistent gripe has been that the negotiations are conducted behind closed doors, with the public and civil society organisations unable to scrutinise the content of the ongoing negotiations. To rejectionist NGOs, this is 'because if people understood its potential impacts, this could lead to widespread opposition' (CEO 2013d). The US organisation Public Citizen thus sees its own campaign as driven by a 'Dracula strategy': 'to drag [trade deals such as TTIP and] TPP into the sunshine so those who will have to live with its consequences can know what's coming and take action' (Wallach 2012). For reformists, the argument on transparency is a slightly different one, although with very similar implications: '[m]ore openness and account-ability' are needed to 'save the talks' from opposition fuelled by the undemocratic manner in which they have been conducted (BEUC 2014d: 1). Moreover, NGOs have consistently criticised the limited value of DG Trade's existing consultation mechanisms, with 'rejectionists' additionally contrasting this to the privi-leged access given to business lobbyists (CEO 2014b). US groups have made similar criticisms, especially of the system of Trade Advisory Committees, which are seen to privilege business inter-ests despite the participation of NGOs (Ingraham and Schneider 2014).

There are of course many other criticisms of TTIP, includ-ing its impact on public services (where the fear often voiced is that the agreement will lead to additional privatisation, or, more accurately, the 'locking-in' of existing privatisation), on intellec-tual property rights or on data privacy (Hilary 2015). But we have focused here on the three issues which we feel have most consist-ently featured in the campaigns of NGOs on TTIP.[14] Together, they have painted a picture of TTIP as a threat to democratic decision-making and regulating in the public interest – not least because of the lack of transparency and accountability in the negotiating process.

The limits to selling TTIP

It is therefore clear that the attempts to depoliticise trade policymaking via the 'economistic' narrative of 'jobs and growth' or the discourse of 'global leadership' have so far failed. While it has spoken of the benefits of investment protection and ISDS as '*a tool for states around the world to attract and maintain FDI* to underpin their economy', or as a means 'to convince its trading partners of the need for clearer and better standards'[15] of investment protection (European Commission 2013i: 3, 4, emphasis in the original), the European Commission has mostly had to emphasise how it hopes to reform the system of investor protection by further protecting the right to regulate; improving the procedures and establishment of arbitration tribunals (notably, making them more transparent and possibly developing a permanent roster of arbitrators); clarifying the relationship of arbitration tribunals to the domestic judiciary; and establishing an appellate mechanism (European Commission 2014f, 2015d).

Admittedly, and in conjunction with the notion that TTIP will allow the EU to 'set global standards' (see chapter 2), these proposals appear to have had an impact on some Social Democrats. The German Economy Minister and Vice-Chancellor, Sigmar Gabriel, put forward proposals for a reformed investor-state arbitration system at a meeting of Social Democratic leaders in Madrid in February 2015. But the principled and fundamental case presented by many groups against the inclusion of ISDS suggests that such a 'reformist' strategy may go only so far in appeasing the opposition. Much of the grassroots of the German Social Democratic Party, for one, remains deeply sceptical of the provision, while the Social Democratic Group in the European Parliament, in its meeting of 4 March 2015, voted to oppose 'the inclusion of ISDS in trade agreements in which other options to enforce investment protection are available' (Socialists and Democrats Group 2015a: 1; *EurActiv* 2015c; Kinkartz 2015).

The Social Democratic Group (on which approval of TTIP relies for support) has of course not adopted an entirely cohesive position on the issue. But, so far, even this equivocation is indicative of an uphill battle for defenders of ISDS, especially as the Social Democrats had previously broadly supported an EP resolution on the opening of TTIP negotiations in May 2013 which was supportive of the agreement and did not single out ISDS for special mention (European Parliament 2013a, 2013b). The EP vote in June 2015 on a TTIP resolution currently being prepared by INTA Chairperson Bernd Lange – who is himself somewhat critical of the provision (see INTA 2015) – may give a better indication of the degree of opposition to ISDS. A number of the other EP committees feeding into the resolution have already given opinions critical of private investor arbitration (e.g., EMPL 2015: 5; ENVI 2015: 12–13). In this climate, several advocates of TTIP have gone as far as to call on the Commission to jettison the provision in order to facilitate the approval of the trade deal (Ikenson 2014; Dullien et al. 2015). Ultimately, the persistent complaint from the Commission – and other advocates – that NGOs have misunderstood the 'technical' purpose of the consultation within the confines of the EU policy process (and labelling their coordinated mass submission as an 'attack'; Wettach 2014) is illustrative of the broad challenge the Commission faces in selling its technocratic view of trade and investment policy in a politicised context.

Similarly, on regulatory convergence, the arguments (which we critiqued in chapters 1 and 2) that 'cutting unnecessary red tape would reduce the cost of doing business', 'be worth billions in new growth for our economies' and lead to 'shared approaches ... likely to be followed around the world' have had far less resonance than the perceived threat of 'chlorinated chicken', 'hormone beef' or the spread of fracking (European Commission 2013b: 2). The *normative* critique of the trading system as serving the interests of big business through a deregulatory agenda has trumped the idea in public discourse that regulation is simply a 'non-tariff barrier' to the free exchange of goods and welfare maximization or that the EU and the US are seeking to shape globalization according to their 'shared values'. The Commission and the USTR's response that there will be no dilution of standards has so far failed to assuage the critics. On one level, it is hard to counter the many instances of potential deregulation highlighted by critics of TTIP by relying on a very narrow set of counter-examples, notably the case of cars (seat belts and headlights) discussed in chapter 3. Moreover, the key negotiating texts remain secret, and there is a perception that business enjoys privileged access to negotiators.

As a result, it could be said that we are seeing a case of the 'bicycle theory' in reverse: while in the past (when trade conflict was largely *distributive*) the lobbying of pro-liberalisation interest groups was seen as key to sustaining the movement towards free trade as a counterweight to protectionism, (big) business lobbying in the case of TTIP appears to fuel suspicion that the negotiations are essentially an 'inside job'. While the Commission and the USTR have also sought to counter this by working to mobilise SMEs in favour of TTIP – trumpeting the benefits of cutting 'red tape' for all businesses, as this 'particularly affects small and medium-sized companies' (European Commission 2014d: 2) – these have so far remained far from enthused. In Germany – where SMEs, or the *Mittelstand*, are considered to be a backbone of the country's export success – only 15 per cent of those polled in one study saw TTIP as creating business opportunities (*Der Spiegel* 2014), while the German SME umbrella group (the Bundesverband mittelständische Wirtschaft) has objected to the inclusion of ISDS in TTIP (BVMW 2014). Meanwhile, UEAPME, the peak association representing SMEs in the EU, while generally expressing its support for TTIP, also has reservations with regard to the agreement's regulatory cooperation dimension. In a hearing at the European Parliament, its director for external relations stated that the UEAPME 'have still to evaluate the (negative) effects on European SMEs and SME policies especially in the field of standardisation' (UEAPME 2014: 3).

This explains why the Commission has, as part of its 'fresh start' to the TTIP negotiations under Malmström, plumped for a new transparency initiative. In her words, 'this agreement needs to be negotiated openly and transparently' and '[e]veryone who is interested must have a chance to comment' (Malmström 2014: 2). That said, 'the price of admission to a discussion as important as this is that you base your arguments on facts, not distortions' (Malmström 2015b: 5). As these excerpts make clear, the hope is to 'kill two birds with one stone' by addressing the criticisms that the TTIP negotiations are undemocratic while also dealing with the perceived 'misinformation' about the negotiations – showing EU citizens (and other interested parties) that they have nothing to fear from the trade deal.

But in our eyes this is unlikely to resolve the *normative* challenge posed by NGOs and their discursive politicisation of TTIP. For one, it does not go far enough in addressing the critique that the negotiations are undemocratic and not transparent; the EU is releasing only its own negotiating texts and not the consolidated agreement text (the actual text being negotiated, which combines proposals from both sides) – as was repeatedly stressed to us in interviews with NGO representatives. The reason given for this – that US negotiators would object to such disclosures – has similarly put the spotlight on the USTR and its policy of limited document release and closed consultation in trade advisory committees. In this NGOs have found support in a European Ombudsman's report on transparency in the TTIP negotiations (the fruit of an investigation into transparency and access to information on TTIP), which spoke of 'the importance of making . . . common negotiating texts available to the EU public before the TTIP agreement is finalised' (European Ombudsman 2015).

Secondly, seeing transparency as a weapon to counter NGO 'myths' and 'horror stories' fundamentally misdiagnoses the problem at hand as one of 'misinformation' rather than of *value-based* opposition to elements (or the entirety) of the TTIP initiative, premised in many cases on detailed analysis of relevant texts. While a less abrasive approach than past instances of Commissioner De Gucht accusing civil society groups of spreading 'lies and misinformation' (cited in De Ville and Siles-Brügge

2014a), it suggests that the Commission has not fundamentally altered its approach to 'selling' TTIP. An opinion piece for *The Guardian* by Malmström and the EU Financial Services Commissioner Jonathan Hill from February 2015 was tellingly entitled 'Don't believe the anti-TTIP hype – increasing trade is a no-brainer'. It repeated the by now standard narrative that TTIP represents 'an adrenaline boost for jobs and growth' and is 'about who will set the global standards for the regulation of goods and services in the 21st century', also emphasising the gains from TTIP to SMEs (Malmström and Hill 2015). The implication of such stark pronouncements, of course, is that those opposed to TTIP are retrograde 'anti-globalists' and 'anti-growth'. But, as the politicisation of TTIP has shown so far, winning the 'hearts and minds' of civil society groups – and retaking the initiative in terms of public discourse – will take far more than showing them a few documents, touting the economic and geostrategic benefits of the agreement, or referring to them as 'liars' and 'scaremongers'.

A successful mobilisation?

In his recent book *How Numbers Rule the World* (2014: 6), Lorenzo Fioramonti argues that 'numbers have been used and abused in governance processes to entrench the power of markets and undermine public debate.' This was precisely the objective behind the econometric studies produced at the behest of the European Commission, an exercise in 'managing fictional expectations'. By reducing regulation to potential non-tariff barriers to trade, these models were also aimed at contributing to the wider process of 'economisation of regulatory politics' we described in chapter 3. Complemented by the argument that TTIP will allow the EU and the US to preserve their 'shared' approach to regulation by setting global standards, these attempts at 'manufacturing consent' for TTIP, however, have clearly not been successful. We have shown how NGOs (so far predominantly in Europe, but also in the US) have stoked a highly contentious public debate about the wider societal impact that TTIP may have. This is largely about *norms* and *values* (touching on the very broad and at the same time 'everyday' issue of how trade agreements affect democratic decision-making and the regulatory choices this produces in the field of social and environmental protection) rather than simply about narrower *distributive* questions (which economic groups win out from freer trade).

This is part of a larger trend, involving the broader shift away from 'embedded liberalism' in the global trade regime and its contestation (e.g., the 'Battle in Seattle'). TTIP, however, goes far beyond existing attempts at 'disembedding' the global trading system and is thus eliciting an even stronger response, in some ways transcending the issue-specific nature of previous campaigning on trade. This is highlighted by the involvement not just of the 'usual suspects' of 'rejectionist' NGOs in the critical debate on TTIP but also of those adopting a more 'reformist' line with respect to the global trading system. Both groups of NGOs have articulated a fairly consistent critique of various elements of the agreement – notably on ISDS, regulatory convergence and transparency – and those in favour of TTIP are clearly worried, calling for more 'political engagement on the highest level' in order to prevent a failure of the negotiations (Lee-Makiyama 2015).

This chapter has thus drawn insights from the literature on 'transnational advocacy networks', which already focused on the politicisation of trade issues by a global network of activists in the late 1990s/early 2000s. But what the case of TTIP calls for is more consideration as to why the politics of global trade and investment appears to be seeing a more effective politicisation and challenge to neoliberal, 'there is no alternative' narratives than other areas of global economic governance, such as global finance or the politics of austerity (Hay and Rosamond 2002; Blyth 2013). In a short, focused book such as this there is of course no space to reflect deeply on why this may be the case. It is, however, interesting to note how civil society activists have identified a clear problem with TTIP and have prescribed a solution in arguing for its defeat – or, at the very least, a radical rethink of its aims. Many NGOs have also linked TTIP to past (and in their eyes entirely successful) struggles against the MAI or WTO (e.g., Global Justice Now 2015) in what appears to be an effort to mobilise activists and resources. Taken together, these elements comprise the three ingredients seen to be crucial to the success of civil society mobilisations in the social movements literature, respectively 'diagnostic', 'prognostic' and 'motivational framing' (Snow and Benford 1988).

It is of course too early to tell what the full effect of the NGO campaign on TTIP will be. The fact that civil society groups often exert pressure through their impact on public opinion (Dür and Mateo 2014) – and thus on elected officials – suggests that TTIP is far from moribund despite the intensive campaigning. Opinion polls suggest that most Europeans still seem to support it – although Germany, which has had one of the most intensive national campaigns against TTIP, is also the place where a majority of people appear to be opposed to a transatlantic trade deal. We cannot really speak of a transnational 'movement' against TTIP, but rather of a more limited advocacy network, which has relied on framing the negotiations in a negative light to put pressure on policymakers.

Despite managing to cut across various issue areas, there are potentially still significant limitations to this strategy. For one, the economic and geostrategic arguments in favour of TTIP we reviewed in chapters 1 and 2 remain quite a powerful force among European Social Democratic parties – on whose support TTIP's approval in the European Parliament may depend, and which also hold a key position in such pivotal Member States as Germany. Not only are they concerned with obtaining jobs and growth for their constituents – there is an affinity between their pan-European narrative against austerity and in favour of greater fiscal expansion and investment (Socialists and Democrats Group 2015b) and the notion that TTIP can act as 'the cheapest stimulus package you can imagine' – but the promise of 'setting global standards' on the basis of Europe's ambitious regulatory model may well appeal to their progressive sensibilities. US Democratic legislators (and civil society groups) are also potentially vulnerable to such arguments. Secondly, the fact that ISDS has emerged as a focal point for much of the campaign is a potential source of weakness, opening the door to a tactical 'dropping' of the issue that might take some of the sting out of the opposition to the agreement. In this vein, the Commission has been mulling the idea of creating a 'permanent investment court' to replace ISDS proceedings – although the exact modalities are still vague at the time of writing (Vincenti 2015). Meanwhile, fears that the agreement will lead to imports of chlorinated chicken and hormone-treated beef can be assuaged by pointing to the 'unassailable' nature of EU food safety standards.

This raises the issue of how likely it is that the present interest in global trade issues will fizzle out, much as it eventually did after the Seattle protests, especially if the TTIP negotiations become very drawn out or amount to very little. As the social movement literature on 'framing' suggests, it is much easier to mobilise in opposition to the imminent threat of a specific agreement than to push for a more complex reform of the global trading system. We turn to this issue, and what it means for the global politics of trade, in the concluding chapter.

Conclusion:
Seizing the TTIP Moment

This book has sought to move beyond the headlines about chlorinated chickens, corporate tribunals and 'growth and jobs' to examine critically the effects and drivers of TTIP. Book title notwithstanding, we of course do not claim to have a definitive answer as to the full effects of TTIP or regarding the 'real', underlying intentions of those pushing for a deal (trade negotiators and business). However, we do believe that we have been able to dissect claims made by both proponents and opponents about the 'true' nature of TTIP. In doing so, we have sought to avoid speculation and have based our analysis on as much official information as is publicly available, supplementing this with interviews and academic and activist secondary literature.

The first two chapters have examined the key narratives used to promote TTIP, namely that it will provide a significant economic boost to the transatlantic economy and that it will help the EU and the US to remain rule-setters for the global economy in the twenty-first century. We concluded that these claims are dubious at best. In chapter 1 we saw how the promise of 'growth and jobs' is based on projections from a form of econometric modelling (computable general equilibrium) whose reputation for forecasting real-world trends is increasingly criticised, even from within the economics profession, especially as similar models in the area of finance failed to predict the 2008 crash (Watson 2014). The TTIP model, in particular, has been fed with data on regulatory convergence that are both unrealistic and biased, overstating the gains from transatlantic liberalisation and downplaying its potential (non-economic) costs. It thus represents an exercise in 'managing fictional expectations' – creating *false* imagined futures that may be difficult to contest for those without the technical expertise to unpick detailed econometric work. Similarly, in chapter 2 we saw that the claim that TTIP is the last opportunity for the EU and the US to set global standards before the rise of emerging economies (and in particular China) is also deeply problematic. The preference of negotiators (and multinational corporations) is for negotiators to adopt bilateral mutual recognition to achieve regulatory convergence – in other words, for the EU and the US to recognise their standards as equivalent only for exporters from either party. This is unlikely to incentivise third parties to adopt EU and US standards – because this represents no advantage with regard to the status quo – and may in fact have the opposite effect of undermining transatlantic regulatory leadership as trade diversion occurs and standards are potentially diluted.

This was the subject of chapter 3, which examined both the drivers and effects of TTIP. Will it completely erode standards of environmental protection, as claimed by critical NGOs, or can ambitious regulatory convergence be reached without lowering environmental, health and labour protections, as is consistently claimed by negotiators? We argued that the mutual recognition approach potentially risks setting into motion a downward spiral, whereby rules on both sides are not undermined *directly* in TTIP (a promise made time and time again by negotiators) but, rather, by enhanced regulatory competition after the agreement is concluded. Moreover, the agreement contains provisions for a 'horizontal' (or cross-cutting) regulatory cooperation chapter that may reinforce trade- and competitiveness tests for regulatory proposals. Both of these dynamics highlight what we see to be the main danger of TTIP: while the agreement may well not contain a direct assault on regulations and cherished public policies, it might contain various provisions that have a 'regulatory chill' effect in the future, including the much criticised ISDS provision, making it easier to deregulate and more difficult to adopt ambitious policies to protect and improve the environment, health or working conditions.

TTIP, not entirely surprisingly, resembles key characteristics and trends in EU and US politics. It shares a depoliticising nature with recent trends in European integration, where decisions are also increasingly delegated to non-elected bodies and away from democratic institutions (Scharpf 1999; Macartney 2014); this may well explain why some of the anti-TTIP sentiment has been tinged with Euroscepticism. At the same time, with TTIP, the power of economic interest groups in EU regulatory policymaking may be enhanced, rendering it more like the US system. There are also important parallels between TTIP and the EU's REFIT programme, which seeks to reduce regulatory and administrative burdens for business. Both paint regulation in a negative light, as a potential (trade) 'barrier' or 'red tape' to be cut as much as possible. *This is our main conclusion about TTIP*: it is driven by both a philosophy and a discourse that idealise the efficient operation of markets and seek to minimise the constraints imposed by democratic decision-making in public policy, which is seen as inherently susceptible to capture by special interests and hence inefficient policy outcomes. This is a dominant assumption in neoclassical economics ('the policy ineffectiveness proposition') as well as in the 'public choice' school of political science, one of the mainstream approaches to the study of regulatory and trade politics (more on which below; on public choice, see Hay 2004). Therefore, there is a consistency between the mainstream economic model produced at the start of the TTIP negotiations and the content of these talks: both are essentially about the desirability of disciplining regulations and, by extension, public policy as much as possible. They are both based on the 'fictional expectation' of creating a perfect market.

But, while the TTIP agenda so far clearly does represent the interests of those who wish to depoliticise trade and regulatory politics, chapter 4 has shown us that there are clear limits to such an agenda. Civil society groups (especially those in Europe) have been at the heart of a fierce campaign against many of these aspects of TTIP and the agreement as a whole. They have underscored how the agreement threatens to undermine democratic decision-making by enshrining private investor rights, highlighted how TTIP may dilute of levels of social and environmental protection, and taken issue with the level of secrecy adopted in the talks. This has resulted in the suspension of negotiations on one of the most controversial aspects of the agreement, ISDS, led policymakers to tone down their proposals for a horizontal regulatory cooperation chapter, and provoked an unprecedented 'transparency initiative' that has seen the release of most EU negotiating proposals. While we should not overstate the extent of the challenge faced by TTIP from civil society – it is still too early to tell what the full impact of the civil society campaign will be – we believe that TTIP should therefore prompt a rethinking of our analysis of global trade politics while potentially opening up possibilities for reshaping it in a more progressive vein.

Rethinking global trade politics

As noted above, the dominant paradigm to understanding global trade politics comes from the public choice school of political science and its emphasis on the rent-seeking behaviour of organised economic interests, which gets in the way of the efficient operation of markets (on this, see Hiscox 2002; Destler 2005). In the context of trade policy, these perceived inefficiencies have a particularly totemic quality, namely the misdiagnosis that protectionism – and notably the 1930 Smoot–Hawley Tariff Act which substantially raised US tariffs – caused the Great Depression and also led to a particular set of domestic trade policies. As one of the doyens of American Political Science, E. E. Schattschneider, put it, the problem was that the Act was 'politically invincible'. This was because 'the pressures [on Congress] supporting the tariff are made overwhelming by the fact that the opposition is negligible' (Schattschneider 1935: 285). The renowned political scientist Mancur Olson (1965) was to put flesh on the bones of Schattschneider's idea by articulating the now well-known 'logic of collective action'. Only economic groups were likely to mobilise politically, given the costs of mobilisation in terms of time and resources. Moreover, given that such a mobilisation was likely to take place only once a clear common economic interest had emerged, protectionists were more likely than exporters or consumer groups to influence trade policy (with non-economic interest groups such as NGOs unlikely to mobilise effectively); the losses from import competition are always easier to identify than the gains from free trade to consumers and exporters. From this understanding of trade politics followed two policy recommendations. Firstly, trade policymakers had to be insulated from protectionist 'special interests'. Enter 'fast track' in the US and the delegation of trade policymaking to a supranational entity in the EU (Destler 2005; Meunier 2005). Secondly, a means had to be found to motivate exporters to lobby for trade liberalisation as a counterweight to protectionists, prompting the 'bicycle theory' we discussed earlier in this book – the idea that liberalisation through reciprocal concessions via trade agreements had to be sustained ('pedalling forward') in order to prevent a return to protectionism ('falling off your bike').

We take issue here with both this analysis and its policy prescription. On the former, chapter 4 showed that the key to understanding the contestation of TTIP was to move away from the idea – quite obvious in the literature we have reviewed in the preceding paragraph – that trade politics is primarily about *distributive* questions. Rather than see economic interests fight it out for the spoils of liberalising (or not liberalising) transatlantic trade, TTIP has involved a fairly united business constituency face-off with civil society groups objecting to the agreement's wider impact on socioeconomic objectives (and the regulations and policy processes designed to achieve them). We referred to this as *normative* trade conflict because it was about deeper *values* and principles, about the 'everyday' politics of the global economy (see Hobson and Seabrooke 2007), making it much harder to defuse by appealing (as advocates of TTIP did) to 'growth and jobs' or 'global economic leadership'. In some ways this form of trade conflict is far more conflictual, given that it centres on more emotive, value-based questions (*pace* Woll and Artigas 2007). What this suggests to our minds is that we need not only to take a broader view of which actors matter in trade policy but also to consider the important role played by ideas in the making of trade policy. In particular, rather than take the view that trade policy is the result of competition between rational, economic actors, we join others in pointing to the important role of framing in legitimating and supporting the adoption of par-ticular trade policies (Wilkinson 2014; Hurt et al. 2013). Notably, the limits to the trade liberalisation 'bicycle' in the case of TTIP – where the consistent mobilisation of businesses in favour of the agreement has fuelled suspicions of a corporate 'inside job' – underscores the importance of discursive framing over 'collective action dynamics'.

Understanding trade conflict as *normative* (rather than purely distributive) is also linked to our critique of the policy prescrip-tions of public choice accounts of trade policymaking. The idea that setting trade policy is best left to depoliticised, technocratic entities (such as the USTR or the European Commission) is especially problematic in our eyes if we consider the profound implications of the 'deep liberalisation' agenda implied by an agreement such as TTIP. As we have argued, this threatens to undermine democratic decision-making by 'economising regulatory politics' and subordinating this to the imperatives of markets. Moreover, if the intention is for TTIP to become 'post-democracy' in its purest form, as argued by Colin Crouch (2014), this depends on going about business as usual.

In this vein, it is heartening to see that there have been moves towards greater transparency on the EU side (most notably, the release of a number of negotiating texts). This will be hard to undo in future. While such moves are for now limited to TTIP, there is considerable pressure from civil society activists to increase both the *depth* of transparency (by releasing the actual, 'consolidated' text of the agreement as it is being negotiated) and its *breadth* (by having the new transparency cover *all* trade agreements and trade policy decisions). On the issue of depth, they have had support from the European Ombudsman (see chapter 4), while on the issue of breadth support has come from (among others) an unlikely quarter, the European People's Party Vice Coordinator in the International Trade Committee, a fierce defender of TTIP and ISDS (Fjellner 2015a, 2015b).

But transparency matters little if no one is watching and holding policymakers to account. Sustaining an interest in global trade issues is therefore crucial if we want to reform the current trading system (with all of its attendant problems; see for example, Wilkinson 2014), especially if we consider that previous campaigns against 'deep trade liberalisation' at the multilateral level faded away only to see these issues reappear (in a more intense form) in bilateral negotiations such as those to establish TTIP. We would hope that, having invested time, energy and personnel in monitoring TTIP, NGOs and others will remain interested and active in trade policy beyond these specific negotiations. Moreover, derailing the TTIP talks will not, on its own, produce a paradise of sustainable and fair trade. But how might the momentum generated by TTIP be seized upon to change trade politics in a more progressive vein?

At the service of citizens

After having fulfilled our *negative function* as academics, critically examining the problems with TTIP, should we also try to perform the *positive function* of coming up with alternatives (Bourdieu 2003)? To do this justice would require an entirely separate book on TTIP or even on trade policy more generally. That said, below we offer some very preliminary thoughts about how this agreement, and trade policy in general, might be put 'at the service of citizens', as European Trade Commissioner Cecilia Malmström herself put it at her confirmation hearing before the European Parliament (2014).

A starting point might be to question whether, by already having invested (at the time of writing) about 200 full-time personnel and 1,500 negotiation hours in further liberalising trade and investment, the EU and the US are really getting their priorities right. The logic behind TTIP is that EU–US 'bilateral trade is not fulfilling its potential' and that there is untapped trade and investment opportunity, but in 2011 annual trade in goods and services already stood at about €702.6 billion and the bilateral investment stock at €2.35 billion (European Commission 2013a: 9, 12). Of course, trade can always be increased by further specialisation and sending (parts of) goods across the Atlantic, but the question is how much this would truly improve the well-being of citizens (the figures generated by the models we discussed in chapter 1, even if taken at face value, suggest only very modest improvements). There might arguably be other, more pressing priorities for transatlantic cooperation than trade and investment. Imagine all the resources, personnel and time spent on TTIP being dedicated to the joint fight against climate change, or tax evasion and unfair tax competition, for decent work and decent wages, less inequality . . . take your pick!

The likely response of TTIP advocates is that this is a *trade* agreement and therefore not the place to tackle such challenges. Trade agreements are about *trade* issues and should not be overburdened with other issues. This view is often shared by opponents of TTIP who, mostly for *normative* reasons, argue that trade agreements should stay away from issues of environmental or social protection. While we have some sympathy for this position, the problem is that trade agreements *already* go far beyond issues of trade, strictly defined. TTIP is the example *par excellence* of this trend. Tariffs – the traditional focus of trade negotiations – are a relatively minor part of the negotiations. As we have shown in this book, TTIP is primarily about domestic regulations that are (often very broadly) seen as having an effect on trade. In a globalised and interdependent world, almost every regulation can be seen as affecting international trade in one way or another and can thus be subsumed under the remit of trade agreement talks as a potential 'non-tariff barrier'.

As a result, it is very one-sided to say that TTIP should ensure that domestic regulation is adjusted to the requisites of international trade, but that it should not be expected to contribute to other non-trade objectives such as fighting climate change. In our opinion, *this inconsistency should be laid bare*. The mobilisation on TTIP might really have a transformative effect on EU, US and global trade politics if NGOs and (progressive) politicians succeed in changing how trade policy is seen from a policy area aimed at removing barriers to trade (in pursuit of the 'imagined global free market') towards an instrument to protect and promote societal preferences in the global market. Rather than facing a situation where too much domestic policy autonomy choice hollows out the full potential of free trade, we are facing a situation where too much free trade is hollowing out domestic policy choices. This may itself, in the longer run, even undermine support for an open global trading system (Polanyi 1944; Rodrik 2011).

As a result, what we need is a change of tack when it comes to TTIP. This might involve the EU and the US deciding to eliminate regulatory differences by consistently *harmonising upwards*. They could also agree to levy taxes at the border that would level the playing field in social, environmental and other areas not only among themselves but also with the rest of the world, which would prevent businesses from relocating to profit from laxer policies and discipline governments through regulatory competition.[1] Both of these moves would be more genuinely in line with the narrative that TTIP could bring growth and jobs and global standards without lowering levels of protection – but neither is currently on the cards. Similarly, rather than using TTIP to expand the reach of the investor arbitration by including provisions on ISDS, the public debate it has sparked could be seized upon to catalyse broader changes to the global investor protection regime. After all, this is an area which has been much criticised by academics, activists and even some policymakers, but which unfortunately has largely existed in relative obscurity. Possible reforms to this system might involve curtailing access to such tribunals for foreign investors and more clearly spelling out their obligations with regard to host states and societies. While we do not claim to have a fully defined answer as to how to remake the global trading system, we hope that these initial reflections – and the TTIP negotiations that sparked them – can sustain a broader debate about the role that trade policymaking should play within society.

Three scenarios for TTIP

We foresee three potential scenarios for TTIP – although these should be treated with caution (in line with our argument in chapter 1 about fictional expectations). The first is that TTIP fails for one of two reasons. Firstly, it could happen during the negotiations, with big business losing interest as the level of ambition is increasingly lowered due to opposition from civil society and sceptical politicians. Secondly, TTIP could fail to clear the ratification hurdle after the conclusion of the negotiations because Congress, the European Parliament or EU Member States (and potentially their national parliaments) are unhappy with the final package deal. In both cases, the root cause of failure would be that the expected benefits of the deal are insufficient to mobilise support against the opposition. This might represent a tactical victory for opponents to TTIP but would hardly constitute a strategic victory, as the global trading system (with all of its acknowledged flaws) would remain in place. From the perspective of the NGOs involved, opposing TTIP cannot be an end in itself.

A second possibility is that TTIP is successfully concluded and ratified because negotiators have adopted a strategy of compromising on some of the most politically sensitive issues (such as ISDS – which might be further reformed or even completely abandoned – and/or a firm commitment not to import 'hormone beef' or 'chlorinated chicken') while preserving key elements from a business perspective (e.g., a 'horizontal' regulatory cooperation chapter). This would be a real Pyrrhic victory for opponents of TTIP, as it would leave a trade deal with many potential negative effects (minus a few highly contested issues) in terms of regulatory depoliticisation.

A third scenario – which we admittedly find the least likely ourselves – is that the NGOs lobbying against TTIP succeed in fundamentally changing the terms of the debate and negotiations such that trade policy becomes an instrument to achieve other policy goals (especially on inter- and transnational issues, such as the fight against climate change and tax evasion). A prerequisite for that would be that NGOs cooperate much more than they do today across the Atlantic and that they engage in profound constructive discussions about how to make the global trading system serve other policy objectives. Before we even get to that stage, more attention to and mobilisation on TTIP is required in the US, where the issue has not yet reached the political maturity it has in the EU. We hope our book may at least make a small contribution in this regard.

Notes

Introduction

1 Or at least not directly. We explain the possible indirect, deregulatory effects of TTIP in chapter 3.

2 Australia, Brunei, Canada, Chile, Japan, Malaysia, Mexico, New Zealand, Peru, Singapore and Vietnam.

3 Throughout this book, we use the concepts 'rules', 'regulations' and 'standards' interchangeably. While there are some notable differences between regulations, which are mandatory, and standards, which are voluntary, standards are, at least in the EU, often referred to in mandatory legislation and therefore resemble regulations. Moreover, we believe that most of the issues we discuss in this book with regard to 'regulatory cooperation' (the negotiators use the overarching concept themselves) apply similarly to both regulations and standards.

4 A qualified majority in the Council normally requires a majority of Member States representing at least three-fifths of the EU's population. While the Treaty of Lisbon stipulates qualified majority voting as the normal rule for trade agreements,

Member States can still ask for unanimity voting if they claim that the cultural diversity within the EU or their ability to provide educational, health or social services is threatened.

Chapter 1   Growth and Jobs

1 More formally, this is known as the Arrow–Debreu theorem.
2 What is more, the Sonnenschein–Mantel–Debreu theorem demonstrates axiomatically (that is, in terms of its own, highly mathematical logic) that individual market equilibria cannot be upscaled to a general, unique equilibrium point (Watson 2014: 22–4).
3 Pareto efficiency is defined as a situation where an actor's welfare can be improved only at the expense of someone else's and is the hallmark of allocative efficiency, maximising the productive use of resources in an economy in mainstream economic thinking.
4 We owe thanks to Jean-Christoph Graz for helping to clarify this point.
5 Personal email communication with one of the authors, 10 April 2014.
6 There are also moves to negotiate an SME chapter within the agreement, although (if we consider the EU's proposal on this) its scope appears to be limited to creating a new committee to consider SME issues as well as a web-based 'helpdesk' providing information on US import and investment procedures (European Commission 2015c).

Chapter 2   Setting Global Standards

1 In this chapter we focus on the argument that TTIP will allow the EU and the US to set the regulatory standards for the twenty-first century, an explicit goal of policymakers on both sides. TTIP has also been interpreted from a security or balance-of-power perspective (as an 'economic NATO' to

guard against the threat posed by China and/or Russia). We touch upon this issue only in passing. Similarly, the question of how TTIP might affect the multilateral trading system centred on the WTO is an interesting issue to which we cannot do justice in a short book such as this.

2 Interviews with European Commission officials, Brussels, December 2014.

3 Sometimes, 'regulatory equivalence' is used as an alternative term for mutual recognition. In both cases, parties decide that their levels of protection are equivalent based on an evaluation of the outcome of regulation. Mostly, regulatory equivalence refers to the acceptance as equivalent of a regulatory framework or system for a type of good or service as a whole (for example, a regulatory regime for credit rating agencies).

4 In this vein, let us not forget that, until recently, observers and practitioners alike argued that the EU and the US have different visions about the appropriate scope of regulatory action.

5 Interviews with European Commission officials, Brussels, December 2014.

Chapter 3   The Bottom Line

1 An important issue that we cannot discuss at sufficient length in this book is how liberalisation strengthens the position of employers, investors and shareholders. This is because it allows them more credibly to threaten trade unions and governments with relocating their investments (increasing their 'exit option') if proposed wage and labour agreements, taxes or regulations raise their costs of doing business and hence lower their profitability. In this way, 'negative' integration (the removal of barriers to trade and capital movements) without also some 'positive' economic integration (creating joint institutions that may upscale taxation and regulation) has a disciplining effect on labour and governments. In this

chapter, we focus on the disciplines specific to TTIP that come on top of the general disciplining effect of FTAs.

2   Another main difference is the timing of impact assessment. In the EU this takes place *before* the regulatory proposal (by the Commission), which is subsequently debated (and can be significantly changed) by the legislators, while in the US the IA has to be done by the agency *at the time of* deciding on the regulation (O'Connor Close and Mancini 2007: 8).

3   At the time of writing, the European Commission was revising its internal Impact Assessment Guidelines. The resolution adopted by the European Parliament on this revision in November 2014 urged reforms that would make the Commission's IAs more similar to those of the US. For example, the (already existent) Impact Assessment Board (IAB) would in the future have to give a positive opinion on an impact assessment before a proposal can be adopted. In December 2014, the European Commission announced that the IAB would be renamed the Regulatory Scrutiny Board and be able to review existing regulations in a 'fitness check', calling upon the Commission to revise or withdraw rules. This is coming close to the scrutiny functions of the OIRA.

4   These are Eurochambres, the European Services Forum (ESF), the European Association of Craft, Small and Medium-Sized Enterprises (known by its French acronym, UEAPME), the Transatlantic Business Council, the Transatlantic Policy Network (TPN), the American Chamber of Commerce to the EU (AmCham EU) and the European Council of American Chambers of Commerce (AmChams in Europe).

5   To some extent, similar provisions can be found in other 'new generation' bilateral trade agreements concluded or being negotiated by the EU and the US. However, the level of ambition in TTIP in terms of the sectoral and horizontal regulatory cooperation commitments is unprecedented.

6   One top US trade official even stated explicitly that '[t]he US is

using transatlantic trade negotiations to push for a fundamental change in the way business regulations are drafted in the EU to allow business groups greater input earlier in the process' (cited in Donnan 2014; see also Myant and O'Brien 2015).

7 Here and elsewhere we refer to the regulatory systems and levels of protection at both the supranational and the Member State level.

8 On the webpage of the American Federation of Labor and Congress of Industrial Organizations (AFL-CIO) (2015) dedicated to TTIP we can read that, 'in many respects, the European nations' social programs to protect families and the environment exceed those of U.S. laws and regulations – and any U.S.-EU agreement must not be used as a tool to deregulate or drive down these higher standards.'

9 Similar concerns have been expressed even more vocally with regard to TPP.

10 It has been remarked that it is somewhat suspicious that this same case is so frequently cited (Moody 2015), as it suggests that negotiators may be struggling to come up with further examples of areas of regulation where most people might agree that protection levels across the Atlantic are equivalent.

11 As one official in DG Trade told us, several of the areas identified by joint industry submissions to the High Level Working Group as 'easy' opportunities for regulatory alignment were found to be irreconcilable (or very difficult to align) once the regulators involved were consulted during the negotiations. Interview with a European Commission official, Brussels, December 2014.

12 The European Council's endorsement of REFIT in October 2013 was accompanied by a report presented by UK Prime Minister David Cameron (and undertaken by his Business Taskforce) entitled *Cut EU Red Tape*. Cameron (2013) praised the European Council conclusions as being 'very strong on deregulation'.

13 This involves a comprehensive policy evaluation assessing

whether the regulatory framework for a particular policy sector is 'fit for purpose'. It implies an evidence-based analysis to check whether EU actions are proportionate to their objectives and delivering expected outcomes.

14 The new Juncker Commission has immediately put the priority it gives to the better regulation agenda into practice. In its 2015 programme, it announced the withdrawal of eighty proposals while initiating only twenty-three (European Commission 2014k). Although Vice-President Timmermans has been stressing that better regulation does not equal deregulation, MEPs from all over the political spectrum have disagreed (see Keating 2014).

15 Another similarity between TTIP and REFIT is how, increasingly, SMEs have been singled out as major beneficiaries of both initiatives.

16 Meanwhile Stoiber has also been appointed as a special advisor to Timmermans.

17 The 'smoking gun' was an internal European Commission email from the US/Canada policy officer in DG Energy reporting that '[t]he US Mission informed us formally that the US authorities have concerns about the transparency and process, *as well as substantive concerns* about the existing proposal' (cited in Friends of the Earth Europe and Transport and Environment 2014: 13, emphasis added).

18 Bulgaria, the Czech Republic, Estonia, Latvia, Lithuania, Poland, Romania, Slovakia and Croatia (Poulsen et al. 2013: 31).

19 This is defined as rules about the process of regulation that 'manage the tensions between the "social" and "economic" goals of regulatory politics, tensions that enflame passionate and highly wrought political conflict over the ethical limits of global capitalism' (Morgan 2003: 488).

20 Interviews with European Commission officials, Brussels, December 2014.

Chapter 4   Challenging TTIP

1 The term 'civil society' is considered by some to be quite nebulous, defined more by what it is not – the state or business – than what it is; that being said, Jan-Aart Scholte (2001: 6) provides a helpful definition in describing it as 'a political space where voluntary associations explicitly seek to shape the rules (in terms of specific policies, wider norms and deeper social structures) that govern one or the other aspect of social life'. Of course, this leaves some ambiguities, as the line between some types of civil society actors such as research institutes and NGOs can be quite blurred (Bellmann and Gerster 1996), but it does point to the important political *advocacy* undertaken by such groups for non-economic motives.

2 Interviews with NGO representatives, Brussels, December 2014.

3 Ibid.

4 For a full list of members, see S2B (2015).

5 Interview with an NGO representative, Brussels, 10 December 2014.

6 Germany has been one of the pioneers of ISDS in its own bilateral investment treaties and has been involved in turf battles with the European Commission over the extension of EU negotiating competence on this issue following the Treaty of Lisbon, in part because of a concern that an EU approach might dilute the investment protections it has already secured. These ongoing struggles over negotiating authority on investment issues may therefore also be a factor in shaping the German position – as are struggles within the German Social Democratic Party (junior party to the Christian Democrats in Germany's grand coalition government) whose grassroots membership is very much opposed to ISDS (Kinkartz 2015).

7 The hearing was overshadowed by the 'cloak-and-dagger'

story of Juncker's *chef de cabinet*, Martin Selmayr, allegedly altering Malmström's written responses so as to suggest that ISDS would be removed from CETA and TTIP, a policy move that the Commissioner designate strenuously denied (De Gruyter 2014).

8 At the time of writing (May 2015) it had still not been formally signed.

9 Interviews with NGO representatives, Brussels, December 2014.

10 Interviews with NGO representatives and European Commission officials, Brussels, December 2014.

11 For example, the link between trade and intellectual property that became embodied in the WTO TRIPS Agreement was in large part the result of US business groups strategically deploying a narrative that 'emphasized the centrality of intellectual property-based goods and services to U.S. competitiveness' and economic performance (Sell and Prakash 2004: 159).

12 Interviews with NGO representatives, Brussels, December 2014.

13 On the cost of suits, see Friends of the Earth Europe (2014a).

14 The issue of public services, for example, has been prominent mainly in the UK, given its association with the NHS.

15 The implicit target of such remarks is often China, with whom the EU is currently negotiating an investment agreement. The argument is that it would likely be unwilling to sign up to ISDS in this agreement if the EU did not include it in TTIP, but this ignores the fact that China has become an avid user of such provisions as it becomes an increasingly important foreign investor in its own right (Poulsen and Berger 2015).

Conclusion

1 To counter the predictable accusation that this amounts to 'selfish protectionism', the EU and the US could decide to allocate revenues from such border taxes to projects in developing countries to help them, for example, in mitigating or adapting to climate change or developing social security systems.

References

Ackerman, F. (2004) 'Still dead after all these years: interpreting the failure of general equilibrium theory', in F. Ackerman and A. Nadal (eds), *The Flawed Foundations of General Equilibrium: Critical Essays on Economic Theory*. Abingdon: Routledge, pp. 14–32.

AFL-CIO (2015) 'U.S.–EU Free Trade Agreement (TTIP)', www.aflcio.org/Issues/Trade/U.S.-EU-Free-Trade-Agreement-TTIP.

Alemanno, A. (2014) *The Transatlantic Trade and Investment Partnership and the Parliamentary Dimension Of Regulatory Cooperation*, Study for the Directorate-General for External Policies, Directorate B, Policy Department. Brussels: European Parliament.

Alternative Trade Mandate (2013) 'Towards an alternative trade mandate for the EU', www.alternativetrademandate.org/wp-content/uploads/2012/06/ATM-Vision-Paper.pdf.

AmChamEU (2008) 'AmCham EU's comments on the EC–OMB Joint draft report on the review of the application of EU and US regulatory impact assessment guidelines on the analysis of impacts on international trade and investment', Position Paper,

29 February, https://www.whitehouse.gov/sites/default/files/omb/assets/omb/inforeg/trade/7.pdf.

American Chambers of Commerce to the European Union (2014) *Together for Jobs and Growth: The Transatlantic Trade and Investment Partnership*. Brussels: AmChams in Europe; www.amcham.hr/files/137/ace-ttip.pdf

Asian Trade Centre (2015) 'The TTIP paper conundrum: A4 versus US letter', 4 February, www.asiantradecentre.org/talkingtrade/2015/2/4/the-ttip-paper-conundrum-a4-versus-us-letter.

Barroso, J. M. D. (2014) Speech by President Barroso at the US Chamber of Commerce, Washington, DC, 30 April, http://europa.eu/rapid/press-release_SPEECH-14-350_en.htm.

Basedow, R. (2014) 'Business lobbying and international investment agreements: the bureaucratic politics behind the international investment regime', paper presented to the European Trade Study Group Annual Conference, Munich, 11–13 September.

Bauer, M. (2015) 'The spiral of silence – how anti-TTIP groups dominate German online media and set the tone for TTIP opinion', 28 January, European Centre for International Political Economy, www.ecipe.org/blog/anti-ttip-german-online-media/.

BBC News (2013) 'EU and US "in Biggest Trade Deal"', 17 June, www.bbc.co.uk/news/business-22943170.

BDI (2008) 'Response to the draft joint report on the review of the application of European Union and United States regulatory impact assessment guidelines on the analysis of impacts on international trade and investment', Position Paper, 8 February, https://www.whitehouse.gov/sites/default/files/omb/assets/omb/inforeg/trade/3.pdf.

Beckert, J. (2013a) 'Imagined futures: fictional expectations in the economy', *Theory and Society*, 42(2): 219–40.

Beckert, J. (2013b) 'Capitalism as a system of expectations: toward a sociological microfoundation of political economy', *Politics and Society*, 41(3): 323–50.

Bellmann, C., and Gerster, R. (1996) 'Accountability in the World Trade Organization', *Journal of World Trade*, 30(6): 31–74.

Bergkamp, L., and Kogan, L. (2013) 'Trade, the precautionary principle, and post-modern regulatory process: regulatory convergence in the Transatlantic Trade and Investment Partnership', *European Journal of Risk Regulation*, 4(4): 493–507.

Bertelsmann and IFO (2013) *Transatlantic Trade and Investment Partnership: Who Benefits from a Free Trade Deal*. Berlin and Munich: Bertelsmann Stiftung and IFO Institute; www.bfna.org/publication/transatlantic-trade-and-investment-partnership-ttip-who-benefits-from-a-free-trade-deal.

BEUC (2014a) 'Consumers at the heart of the Transatlantic Trade and Investment Partnership (TTIP)', BEUC Position Statement, BEUC-X-2014-031, 21 May, Brussels: BEUC.

BEUC (2014b) 'How will TTIP affect the health of Europeans?', 11 September, www.beuc.eu/blog/how-will-ttip-affect-the-health-of-europeans/.

BEUC (2014c) 'TTIP: investment protection and ISDS – BEUC response to the European Commission's public consultation', BEUC Position Statement, BEUC-X-2014-050, 4 July. Brussels: BEUC.

BEUC (2014d) 'Transparency and engagement in the TTIP: how to improve EU trade negotiators' accountability to the public', BEUC Position Statement, BEUC-X-2014-080, Brussels: BEUC.

BEUC (2015) 'What we think of TTIP', www.beuc.eu/blog/ttip/.

BEUC and Friends of the Earth Europe (2014) 'Letter to Commissioner De Gucht: communication of the results of the TTIP economic impact assessment', 5 May, www.beuc.eu/publications/beuc-x-2014-036_mgo_joint_letter_to_mr_de_gucht_on_economic_figures-final.pdf.

Blyth, M. (2009) 'Torn between two lovers? Caught in the middle of British and American IPE', *New Political Economy*, 14(3): 329–36.

Blyth, M. (2013) *Austerity: The History of a Dangerous Idea.* Oxford: Oxford University Press.

Böhringer, C., and Löschel, A. (2006) 'Computable general equilibrium models for sustainability impact assessments: status quo and prospects', *Ecological Economics,* 60(1): 49–64.

Bourdieu, P. (2003) *Firing Back: Against the Tyranny of the Market 2.* London: Verso.

British American Business (2015) *Local, Specific, Tangible: How a EU–US Trade and Investment Agreement Can Help Businesspeople and their Companies in the UK.* London: British American Business; http://issuu.com/babnewyork/docs/local__specific__tangible/0.

BUSINESSEUROPE (2014) 'Why TTIP matters to European business', 14 April, www.businesseurope.eu/Content/Default.asp?pageid=568&docid=32927.

BUSINESSEUROPE and US Chamber of Commerce (2012) 'Regulatory cooperation in the EU–US economic agreement', http://ec.europa.eu/enterprise/policies/international/cooperating-governments/usa/jobs-growth/files/consultation/regulation/9-business-europe-us-chamber_en.pdf.

BUSINESSEUROPE, Eurochambres, UAEMPE, ESF, AMCHAM EU, AMCHAMS in Europe, US Chamber of Commerce, Transatlantic Business Council, TPN (2013) 'Business organisations announce alliance for a Transatlantic Trade and Investment Partnership', 16 May, www.transatlanticbusiness.org/wp-content/uploads/2014/11/2013-05-16-Joint-Press-release-on-Alliance-for-TTIP.pdf.

BWMW (2014) 'Stellungnahme im Rahmen des Konsultationsverfahrens der EU-Kommission zum Investitionsschutz im Geplanten Transatlantischen Freihandelsabkommen TTIP', Positionspapier, Berlin: BWMW.

Cafruny, A. W., and Ryner, J. M. (2007) *Europe at Bay: In the Shadow of US Hegemony.* Boulder, CO: Lynne Rienner.

Cameron, D. (2013) 'PM's European Council Press Conference: October 2013', 25 October, https://www.gov.

uk/government/speeches/pms-european-council-press-conf
erence-october-2013.

Capaldo, J. (2014) *The Trans-Atlantic Trade and Investment Partnership: European Disintegration, Unemployment and Instability*, Global Development and Environment Institute Working Paper No. 14-03. Medford, MA: Tufts University.

CEN/CENELEC (2013) 'Position paper on EU–US Transatlantic Trade and Investment Partnership (TTIP) – Technical Barriers to Trade – Initial EU Position Paper', September, Brussels: CEN/CENELEC.

CEO (2013a) 'A transatlantic corporate bill of rights', 3 June, http://corporateeurope.org/trade/2013/06/transatlantic-corp orate-bill-rights.

CEO (2013b) 'Unravelling the spin: a guide to corpo-rate rights in the EU–US trade deal', 9 July, http://corpor ateeurope.org/trade/2013/07/unravelling-spin-guide-corpor ate-rights-eu-us-trade-deal.

CEO (2013c) 'Regulation – none of our business?', 16 December, http://corporateeurope.org/trade/2013/12/regul ation-none-our-business.

CEO (2013d) 'Busting the myths of transparency around the EU–US trade deal', 25 September, http://corporateeurope.org/ trade/2013/09/busting-myths-transparency-around-eu-us-tra de-deal.

CEO (2014a) 'TTIP: debunking the business propaganda over investor rights', 3 July, http://corporateeurope.org/ international-trade/2014/07/ttip-debunking-business-propa ganda-over-investor-rights.

CEO (2014b) 'Who lobbies most on TTIP?', 8 July, http://corporateeurope.org/international-trade/2014/07/who-lobbies-most-ttip.

CEO (2015) 'TTIP investor rights: the many voices ignored by the Commission', 3 February, http://corporateeurope.org/ international-trade/2015/02/ttip-investor-rights-many-voices-ignored-commission.

CEO et al. (2013) 'Letter to Ambassador Michael Froman and Commissioner Karel De Gucht', 16 December, http://corporateeurope.org/sites/default/files/attachments/ttip_investment_letter_final.pdf.

CEPII (2013) 'Transatlantic trade: whither partnership, which economic consequences?', Policy Brief No.1, September, www.cepii.fr/CEPII/fr/publications/pb/abstract.asp?NoDoc=6113.

CEPR (2013) *Reducing Transatlantic Barriers to Trade and Investment: An Economic Assessment.* London: CEPR.

Chang, H.-J. (2014) 'Economics is too important to leave to the experts', *The Guardian*, 30 April, www.theguardian.com/commentisfree/2014/apr/30/economics-experts-economists.

Clark, J. D., and Themudo, N. S. (2006) 'Linking the web and the street: internet-based "dotcauses" and the anti-globalization movement', *World Development*, 34(1): 50–74.

Council of the EU (2013) 'Directives for the negotiation on the Transatlantic Trade and Investment Partnership between the European Union and the United States of America', 17 June, http://data.consilium.europa.eu/doc/document/ST-111 03-2013-DCL-1/en/pdf.

Council of the EU (2014a) 'Outcome of proceedings: working party on information on 17 October 2014', http://data.consilium.europa.eu/doc/document/ST-14713-2014-INIT/en/pdf.

Council of the EU (2014b) 'Council conclusions on TTIP – Foreign Affairs Council (Trade): Brussels, 21 November 2014', www.consilium.europa.eu/uedocs/cms_data/docs/pressdata/EN/foraff/145906.pdf.

Cowles, M. G. (2001) 'The transatlantic business dialogue and domestic business–government relations', in M. G. Cowles, J. A. Caporaso and T. Risse-Kappen (eds), *Transforming Europe: Europeanization and Domestic Change*. Ithaca, NY: Cornell University Press, pp. 159–79.

Crisp, J. (2014) 'Canada tar sands will not be labelled 'dirty' after all', 17 December, *EurActiv*, www.euractiv.com/sections/

energy/canada-tar-sands-will-not-be-labelled-dirty-after-all-310910.

Crouch, C. (2014) 'Democracy at a TTIP'ing point: seizing a slim chance to reassert democratic sovereignty in Europe', *Juncture* 21(3), www.ippr.org/juncture/democracy-at-a-ttiping-point-seizing-a-slim-chance-to-reassert-democratic-sovereignty-in-europe.

Damro, C. (2012) 'Market power Europe', *Journal of European Public Policy*, 19(5): 682–99.

De Gruyter, C. (2014) 'Ruzie over oplossen van ruzies: handelsver-drag Europa–Amerika', 15 October, *NRC Handelsblad*, www.nrc.nl/handelsblad/van/2014/oktober/15/ruzie-over-oploss en-van-ruzies-1428913.

De Gucht, K. (2013a) 'Transatlantic Trade and Investment Partnership (TTIP) – solving the regulatory puzzle', speech delivered at the Aspen Institute Prague Annual Conference, 10 October, http://europa.eu/rapid/press-release_SPEECH-13-801_en.htm.

De Gucht, K. (2013b) 'A European perspective on trans-atlantic free trade', speech delivered at the Harvard Kennedy School, 2 March, http://europa.eu/rapid/press-release_SPEECH-13-178_en.htm.

De Gucht, K. (2014a) 'TTIP: strengthening our values', speech delivered at the Wrocław Global Forum, 6 June, http://europa.eu/rapid/press-release_SPEECH-14-439_en.htm.

De Gucht, K. (2014b) 'Towards the Transatlantic Trade and Investment Partnership: stepping up a gear', speech delivered at the Atlantic Council, Washington, DC, 18 February, http://europa.eu/rapid/press-release_SPEECH-14-140_en.htm.

De Ville, F., and Siles-Brügge, G. (2014a) '"Lies": elections, out-bursts and the EU–US free trade talks', 23 May, *Manchester Policy Blogs*, http://blog.policy.manchester.ac.uk/featured/2014/05/lies-elections-outbursts-and-eu-us-free-trade-talks/.

De Ville, F., and Siles-Brügge, G. (2014b) 'The Transatlantic Trade and Investment Partnership and the role of computable general equilibrium modelling: an exercise in "managing fictional expectations"', *New Political Economy*, doi: 10.1080/13563467.2014.983059.

Defraigne, P. (2013) 'Choosing between Europe and the TTIP', *Madariaga Paper*, 6(7), November. Brussels: Madariaga College of Europe Foundation.

Destler, I. M. (2005) *American Trade Politics*. 4th edn, Washington, DC: Institute for International Economics.

Dixon, P. B., and Rimmer, M. T. (2010) 'Johansen's contribution to CGE modelling: originator and guiding light for fifty years', paper presented to the Symposium in Memory of Professor Leif Johansen, and to celebrate the fiftieth anniversary of the publication of his 'A multi-sectoral study of economic growth', Norwegian Academy of Science and Letters, 20–21 May.

Donnan, S. (2014) 'US pushes for greater transparency in EU business regulation', *Financial Times*, 23 February, www.ft.com/intl/cms/s/0/6e9b7190-9a65-11e3-8e06-00144feab7de.html.

Donnan, S. (2015) 'Obama steps up battle to win fast-track trade deal authority', *Financial Times*, 18 January, www.ft.com/intl/cms/s/0/d8a564aa-9d85-11e4-9b22-00144feabdc0.html.

Donnan, S., and Wagstyl, S. (2014) 'Transatlantic trade talks hit German snag', *Financial Times*, 14 March, www.ft.com/cms/s-/0/cc5c4860-ab9d-11e3-90af-00144feab7de.html.

Dullien, S., Garcia, A., and Janning, J. (2015) 'A fresh start for TTIP', European Council on Foreign Relations (ECFR) Policy Brief, London: ECFR.

Dür, A., and Lechner, L. (2015) 'Business interests and the Transatlantic Trade and Investment Partnership', in J. F. Morin, T. Novotna, F. Ponjaert and M. Télo (eds), *The Politics of Transatlantic Trade Negotiations*. Farnham: Ashgate, pp. 69–80.

Dür, A., and Mateo, G. (2014) 'Public opinion and interest group influence: how citizen groups derailed the Anti-Counterfeiting Trade Agreement', *Journal of European Public Policy*, 21(8): 1199–217.

Eberhardt, P., Redlin, B., and Toubeau, C. (2014) *Trading Away Democracy: How CETA's Investor Protection Rules Threaten the Public Good in Canada and the EU.* Amsterdam and elsewhere: Association Internationale de Techniciens, Experts et Chercheurs et al.

ECIPE (2010) *A Transatlantic Zero Agreement: Estimating the Gains from Transatlantic Free Trade in Goods*, ECIPE Occasional Paper No. 4/2010, Brussels: European Centre for International Political Economy.

The Economist (2007) 'Brussels rules OK: how the European Union is becoming the world's chief regulator', *The Economist*, 20 September.

The Economist (2013) 'The Merkel plan: Germany's vision for Europe is all about making the continent more competitive', *The Economist*, 15 June.

ECORYS (2009a) *Non-Tariff Measures in EU-US Trade and Investment: An Economic Analysis.* Rotterdam: Ecorys Nederland BV.

ECORYS (2009b) *ANNEXES: Non-Tariff Measures in EU-US Trade and Investment: An Economic Analysis.* Rotterdam: Ecorys Nederland BV.

Egan, D. (2001) 'The limits of internationalization: a neo-Gramscian analysis of the Multilateral Agreement on Investment', *Critical Sociology*, 27(3): 74–97.

EMPL (2015) 'Opinion of the Committee on Employment and Social Affairs for the Committee on International Trade on recommendations to the European Commission on the negotiations for the Transatlantic Trade and Investment Partnership (TTIP) (2014/2228(INI))', 1 April, PE546.672v02-00, Brussels: European Parliament.

ENVI (2015) 'Opinion of the Committee on the Environment, Public Health and Food Safety for the Committee on International Trade on Recommendations to the European Commission on the Negotiations for the Transatlantic Trade and Investment Partnership (TTIP) (2014/2228(INI))',

16 April, PE544.393v02-00, Brussels: European Parliament.

ETUC (2013) 'ETUC Position on the Transatlantic Trade and Investment Partnership', www.etuc.org/sites/www.etuc.org/files/EN-ETUC-position-on-TTIP-2_2.pdf.

ETUC and AFL-CIO (2014) 'Declaration of Joint Principles – ETUC/AFL-CIO: TTIP must work for the people, or it won't work at all', www.etuc.org/sites/www.etuc.org/files/document/files/afl-cio_ttip_report_uk_1.pdf.

EU Trade Insights (2015) 'Member States oppose TTIP non-central regulatory cooperation', 28 January, www.vieuws.eu/eutradeinsights/member-states-oppose-ttip-non-central-regulatory-cooperation/.

EurActiv (2013) 'In move towards trade talks, EU to lift ban on some US meats', 5 February, www.euractiv.com/global-europe/move-trade-talks-eu-lifts-ban-us-news-517571.

EurActiv (2014a) 'Germany wants investment clause scrapped in EU–Canada trade deal', 25 September, www.euractiv.com/sections/trade-industry/germany-wants-investment-clause-scrapped-eu-canada-trade-deal-308717.

EurActiv (2014b) 'Anti-TTIP demonstrations seize European capitals', 13 October, www.euractiv.com/sections/trade-society/anti-ttip-demonstrations-seize-european-capitals-309119.

EurActiv (2015a) 'ISDS decision delayed to end of TTIP talks', 13 January, www.euractiv.com/sections/trade-society/isds-decision-delayed-end-ttip-talks-311234.

EurActiv (2015b) 'EU to step up TTIP communication efforts', 16 March, www.euractiv.com/sections/trade-society/eu-step-ttip-communication-efforts-312920.

EurActiv (2015c) 'Malmström: Germany's TTIP debate "more heated"', 24 February, www.euractiv.com/sections/trade-society/malmstrom-germanys-ttip-debate-more-heated-312354.

European Commission (1988) 'Europe 1992: the overall challenge', SEC (88) 524 final, Brussels: European Commission.

European Commission (2005) 'Communication from the Commission to the European Parliament: European values in the globalised world – contribution of the Commission to the October meeting of heads of state and government', 20 October 2005, COM(2005) 525 final, Brussels: European Commission.

European Commission (2007a) 'Commission Staff Working Document – The Single Market: review of achievements', SEC(2007) 1521 final, Brussels: European Commission.

European Commission (2007b) 'Commission Staff Working Document: The external dimension of the Single Market review', SEC(2007) 1519, Brussels: European Commission.

European Commission (2010a) 'Communication from the Commission to the European Parliament, the Council, the Economic and Social Committee and the Committee of the Regions: towards a Single Market Act: for a highly competitive social market economy: 50 proposals for improving our work, business and exchanges with one another', COM(2010) 608 final, Brussels: European Commission.

European Commission (2010b) 'Communication from the Commission: Europe 2020: A European strategy for smart, sustainable and inclusive growth', COM(2010) 2020, Brussels: European Commission.

European Commission (2012) 'External sources of growth: progress report on EU trade and investment relationship with key economic partners', Brussels: European Commission.

European Commission (2013a) 'European Commission Staff Working Document: impact assessment report on the future of EU–US trade relations', SWD(2013) 68 final, Brussels: European Commission.

European Commission (2013b) 'Transatlantic Trade and Investment Partnership: the regulatory part', September, Brussels: European Commission.

European Commission (2013c) 'EU–US Transatlantic Trade and Investment Partnership: trade cross-cutting disciplines and institutional provisions', Initial EU Position Paper, Brussels: European Commission.

European Commission (2013d) 'Issues paper communicating on TTIP: areas for cooperation between the Commission services and Member States', 7 November, Brussels: European Commission; http://corporateeurope.org/trade/2013/11/lea ked-european-commission-pr-strategy-communicating-ttip.

European Commission (2013e) 'Trade: a key source of growth and jobs for the EU: Commission contribution to the European Council of 7–8 February', Brussels: European Commission.

European Commission (2013f) 'Independent study outlines benefits of EU–US trade agreement', press release, 12 March, http://europa.eu/rapid/press-release_MEMO-13-211_en.htm.

European Commission (2013g) 'Note for the attention of the Trade Policy Committee: initial Position Papers on: regulatory issues – cross-cutting disciplines and institutional provisions; technical barriers to trade; regulatory cluster: automotive sector, chemicals, pharmaceuticals; sanitary and phytosanitary issues (sps); trade and sustainable development; anti-trust & mergers, government influence and subsidies; trade and investment in raw materials and energy', m.d. 238/13, 20 June, Brussels: European Commission.

European Commission (2013h) *Transatlantic Trade and Investment Partnership: The Economic Analysis Explained*, September, http://trade.ec.europa.eu/doclib/docs/2013/sept ember/tradoc_151787.pdf.

European Commission (2013i) *Factsheet: Investment Protection and Investor-to-State Dispute Settlement in EU Agreements*, November, http://trade.ec.europa.eu/doclib/docs/2013/nov ember/tradoc_151916.pdf.

European Commission (2014a) 'Commission to consult European public on provisions in EU–US trade deal on investment and investor-state dispute settlement', press release, 21 January, http://europa.eu/rapid/press-release_IP-14-56_en. htm.

European Commission (2014b) 'Communication from the Commission to the European Parliament, the Council, the European Economic and Social Committee and the Committee of the Regions: Regulatory Fitness and Performance Programme (REFIT): state of play and outlook', COM(2014) 0368 final, Brussels: European Commission.

European Commission (2014c) 'The Transatlantic Trade and Investment Partnership (TTIP) regulatory issues: EU position on motor vehicles', 14 May, http://trade.ec.europa.eu/doclib/docs/2014/may/tradoc_152467.pdf.

European Commission (2014d) 'TTIP explained', 19 March, http://trade.ec.europa.eu/doclib/docs/2014/may/tradoc_152 462.pdf.

European Commission (2014e) 'Expert group to advise European Commission on EU–US trade talks', http://europa.eu/rapid/press-release_IP-14-79_en.htm.

European Commission (2014f) *Public Consultation on Modalities for Investment Protection and ISDS in TTIP*, March, http://trade.ec.europa.eu/doclib/docs/2014/march/tradoc_152280.pdf.

European Commission (2014g) 'Online public consultation on investment protection and investor-to-state dispute settlement (ISDS) in the Transatlantic Trade and Investment Partnership Agreement (TTIP)', http://trade.ec.europa.eu/consultations/index.cfm?consul_id=179.

European Commission (2014h) 'Letter: your request for registration of a proposed citizens' initiative entitled "STOP TTIP"', 10 September, http://ec.europa.eu/citizens-initiative/public/documents/2552.

European Commission (2014i) 'Commission to further boost TTIP transparency', 19 November, http://trade.ec.europa.eu/doclib/press/index.cfm?id=1201&title=Commission-to-further-boost-TTIP-transparency.

European Commission (2014j) *Standard Eurobarometer 82: Public Opinion in the European Union: First Results.* Brussels: European Commission.

European Commission (2014k) 'A new start: European Commission work plan to deliver jobs, growth and investment', Press release, 16 December, http://europa.eu/rapid/press-release_IP-14-2703_en.htm.

European Commission (2014l) 'Mission letter: Commissioner for trade', 10 September, http://ec.europa.eu/archives/juncker-commission/docs/malmstrom_en.pdf.

European Commission (2015a) 'Textual proposal: initial provisions for chapter on regulatory cooperation', 10 February, http://trade.ec.europa.eu/doclib/docs/2015/february/tradeoc_153120.pdf.

European Commission (2015b) 'Textual proposal: sanitary and phytosanitary measures', 7 January, Brussels: European Commission.

European Commission (2015c) 'Textual proposal: small and medium-sized enterprises', 7 January, Brussels: European Commission.

European Commission (2015d) 'Commission Staff Working Paper – report: online public consultation on investment protection and Investor-to-State Dispute Settlement (ISDS) in the Transatlantic Trade and Investment Partnership (TTIP)', SWD(2015) 3 final, Brussels: European Commission.

European Commission (2015e) 'European Commission publishes TTIP legal texts as part of transparency initiative', 7 January, http://trade.ec.europa.eu/doclib/press/index.cfm?id=1231.

European Commission (2015f) 'About TTIP – basics, benefits, concerns', http://ec.europa.eu/trade/policy/in-focus/ttip/about-ttip/questions-and-answers/index_en.htm.

European Commission (2015g) 'Textual proposal: initial provisions for chapter on regulatory cooperation', 4 May, http://trade.ec.europa.eu/doclib/docs/2015/april/tradoc_153403.pdf.

European Court of Auditors (2014) *Special Report: Are Preferential Trade Agreements Appropriately Managed?* Luxembourg: European Court of Auditors.

European Ombudsman (2015) 'Decision of the European ombudsman closing her own-initiative inquiry OI/10/2014/RA concerning the European Commission', Brussels: European Ombudsman.

European Parliament (2013a) 'EU trade and investment agreement negotiations with the US', Resolution adopted 23 May, P7_TA(2013)0227, Brussels: European Parliament.

European Parliament (2013b) 'Debates – EU trade and investment agreement negotiations with the US', 22 May, Strasbourg, http://www.europarl.europa.eu/sides/getDoc.do?type=CRE&reference=20130522&secondRef=ITEM-017&language=EN&ring=B7-2013-0187.

European Parliament (2014) 'Hearing of Cecilia Malmström, Commissioner-Designate (Trade)', 29 September, Brussels: European Parliament.

Eurostat (2015) 'Trade in goods, by main world traders', http://ec.europa.eu/eurostat/tgm/table.do?tab=table&init=1&language=en&pcode=tet00018&plugin=1.

Faoila, A. (2014) 'Free trade with U.S.? Europe balks at chlorine chicken, hormone Beef', *Washington Post*, 4 December, www.washingtonpost.com/world/europe/free-trade-with-us-europe-balks-at-chlorine-chicken-hormone-beef/2014/12/04/e9aa131c-6c3f-11e4-bafd-6598192a448d_story.html.

Financial Times (2014) 'Jean-Claude Juncker plays with future of EU–US trade deal', 23 October, www.ft.com/intl/cms/s/0/3571c8b2-5ac0-11e4-b449-00144feab7de.html.

Fioramonti, L. (2014) *How Numbers Rule the World: The Use and Abuse of Statistics in Global Politics*. London: Zed Books.

Fjellner, C. (2015a) 'All trade policy areas would benefit from Malmström's TTIP transparency initiative', *EurActiv*, 18 February, www.euractiv.com/sections/trade-society/all-trade-agreements-would-benefit-malmstroms-ttip-transparency-initiative.

Fjellner, C. (2015b) 'Politik', www.fjellner.eu/politik/.

Foreign and Commonwealth Office (2012) *Review of the Balance of Competences between the United Kingdom and the European Union*, Cm 8415. London: The Stationery Office.

Fox, B. (2015) 'Europe needs TTIP to avoid loss of influence, Germany warns', *EUObserver*, 24 February, https://euobserver.com/news/127768.

Friends of the Earth Europe (2014a) *The Hidden Cost of EU Trade Deals: Investor-State Dispute Settlement Cases Against Member States*. Brussels: Friends of the Earth Europe.

Friends of the Earth Europe (2014b) 'No fracking way: how the EU–US trade agreement risks expanding fracking', Issue Brief, March, www.foeeurope.org/sites/default/files/publications/foee_ttip-isds-fracking-060314.pdf.

Friends of the Earth Europe & Transport and Environment (2014) *Dirty Deals: How Trade Talks Threaten to Undermine EU Climate Policies and Bring Tar Sands to Europe*, July, www.foeeurope.org/sites/default/files/publications/foee-fqd-trade-ttip-170714_0.pdf.

Froman, M. (2014) 'Remarks by Ambassador Michael Froman at the No Labels Business Leaders Forum', speech delivered in Washington, DC, 17 September, https://ustr.gov/about-us/policy-offices/press-office/speeches/2014/September/Remarks-by-Ambassador-Froman-at-No-Labels-Business-Leaders-Forum.

Froman, M. (2015) 'Remarks by Ambassador Michael Froman to the National Association of Counties', speech delivered in Washington, DC, 23 February, https://ustr.gov/about-us/policy-offices/press-office/speechestranscripts/2015/february/remarks-ambassador-michael-0.

Fuller, T. (2002) 'As EU gains in heft, Washington's diplomacy slowly changes', *New York Times*, 20 December, www.nytimes.com/2002/12/20/news/20iht-eu_ed3__2.html.

George, C. (2010) *The Truth About Trade: The Real Impact of Liberalization*. London: Zed Books.

Gill, S. (1995) 'Globalisation, market civilisation and disciplinary neoliberalism', *Millennium: Journal of International Studies*, 24(3): 399–423.

Gill, S. (2000) 'Toward a postmodern prince? The Battle in Seattle as a moment in the new politics of globalisation', *Millennium: Journal of International Studies*, 29(1): 131–40.

Global Justice Now (2015) 'TTIP: a threat to democracy, standards and jobs', www.globaljustice.org.uk/ttip-threat-democracy-standards-and-jobs.

Grant, W. (2007) 'The shift from duopoly to oligopoly in agricultural trade', in D. Lee and R. Wilkinson (eds), *The WTO after Hong Kong: Progress in, and Prospects for, the Doha Development Agenda*. Abingdon: Routledge, pp. 169–86.

Hall, C. (2014) 'Canada to clinch trade deal with EU in September', 31 July, *CBC News*, www.cbc.ca/news/politics/canada-to-clinch-trade-deal-with-eu-in-september-1.2724350.

Hamilton, D. S. (2014) 'America's mega-regional trade diplomacy: comparing TPP and TTIP', *International Spectator: Italian Journal of International Affairs*, 49(1): 81–97.

Hannah, E. R. (2014) 'The quest for accountable governance: embedded NGOs and demand driven advocacy in the international trade regime', *Journal of World Trade*, 48(3): 457–79.

Hanson, B. T. (1998) 'What happened to Fortress Europe: external trade policy liberalization in the European Union', *International Organization*, 52(1): 55–85.

Hay, C. (2004) 'Theory, stylized heuristic or self-fulfilling prophecy? The status of rational choice theory in public administration', *Public Administration*, 82(1): 39–62.

Hay, C., and Rosamond, B. (2002) 'Globalisation, European integration and the discursive construction of economic imperatives', *Journal of European Public Policy*, 9(2): 147–67.

Herman, S., and Chomsky, N. (1988) *Manufacturing Consent: The Political Economy of the Mass Media*. New York: Pantheon Books.

Hilary, J. (2015) *The Transatlantic Trade and Investment Partnership: A Charter for Deregulation, An Attack on Jobs, An End to Democracy*, February. Brussels and London: Rosa Luxemburg Stiftung and War on Want.

Hiscox, M. (2002) *International Trade and Political Conflict: Commerce, Coalitions and Mobility*. Princeton, NJ: Princeton University Press.

HLWG (2013) 'Final Report: High Level Working Group on Growth and Jobs', 11 February, http://trade.ec.europa.eu/doclib/docs /2013/february/tradoc_150519.pdf.

Hobson, J. M., and Seabrooke, L. (eds) (2007) *Everyday Politics of the World Economy*. Cambridge: Cambridge University Press.

Hopewell, K. (2009) 'The technocratization of protest: transnational organizations and the WTO', in D. Fasenfest (ed.), *Engaging in Social Justice*. Leiden: Brill, pp. 161–79.

Horel, S., and CEO (2015) *A Toxic Affair: How the Chemical Lobby Blocked Action on Hormone Disrupting Chemicals*. Brussels: Corporate Europe Observatory.

House of Lords (2013) *Inquiry on Transatlantic Trade and Investment Partnership: Evidence Session No. 2*, 31 October. London: The Stationery Office.

House of Lords (2014) *The Transatlantic Trade and Investment Partnership: European Union Committee, 14th Report of Session 2013-14*. London: The Stationery Office.

Huntington, S. P. (1989) 'The United States: Decline or Renewal?', *Adelphi Papers*, 235, pp. 63–80.

Hurt, S. R., Lee, D., and Lorenz, U. (2013) 'The argumentative dimension to the EPAs', *International Negotiation*, 18(1): 67–87.

Ikenson, D. (2014) 'A compromise to advance the trade agenda: purge negotiations of Investor-State Dispute Settlement', *Cato Institute Free Trade Bulletin*, no. 57, 4 March.

Ingraham, C., and Schneider, H. (2014) 'Industry voices dominate the trade advisory system', *Washington Post*, 27 February, www.

washingtonpost.com/wp-srv/special/business/trade-advi
sory-committees/.

INTA (2015) 'Working document – In view of preparing the draft
report on Parliament's recommendations to the Commission
on the negotiations for the Transatlantic Trade and Investment
Partnership', 9 January, PE546.593, www.ttip2014.eu/files/
content/docs/Full%20documents/lange%20report.pdf.

Jacoby, W., and Meunier, S. (2010) 'Europe and the management
of globalization', *Journal of European Public Policy*, 17(3):
299–317.

Johnston, J., and Laxer, G. (2003) 'Solidarity in the age of globalization: lessons from the anti-MAI and Zapatista struggles',
Theory and Society, 32(1): 39–91.

Jones, E., and Macartney, H. (2015) 'TTIP and the 'finance
exception': venue-shopping and the breakdown of financial regulatory coordination', *Journal of Banking Regulation*
(forthcoming).

Juncker, J.-C. (2014) 'A new start for Europe: my agenda for jobs,
growth, fairness and democratic change: political guidelines
for the next European Commission', opening statement in the
European Parliament Plenary Session, Strasbourg, 22 October,
Brussels: European Commission.

Kagan, R. (2004) *Of Paradise and Power: America and Europe in
the New World Order*. New York: Alfred A. Knopf.

Keating, D. (2014) 'Commission to scrap air and waste proposals', *European Voice*, 11 December, www.europeanvoice.com/
article/juncker-to-scrap-air-and-waste-proposals/.

Keck, M. E., and Sikkink, K. (1998) *Activists beyond Borders:
Advocacy Networks in International Politics*. Ithaca, NY: Cornell
University Press.

Kinkartz, S. (2015) 'German Social Democrats fear free
trade', *Deutsche Welle*, 23 February, www.dw.de/german-
social-democrats-fear-free-trade/a-18275595.

Kosinska, M., Murray, J., Möller, H. R., and Renshaw, N. (2014)
'Dissenting opinion', http://ec.europa.eu/smart-regulation/

refit/admin_burden/docs/annex_12_en_hlg_ab_dissenting_
opinion.pdf.

Krugman, P. (2014) 'No big deal', *New York Times*, 27 February,
www.nytimes.com/2014/02/28/opinion/krugman-no-big-de
al.html.

Lang, A. (2011) *World Trade Law after Neoliberalism: Re-imagining
the Global Economic Order*. Oxford: Oxford University
Press.

Lauer, S., and Ducourtieux, C. (2015) 'Traité transat-
lantique: l'Europe dans l'attente d'une accélération
américaine', *Le Monde*, 20 April, www.lemonde.fr/economie/
article/2015/04/20/traite-transatlantique-l-europe-dans-l-atten
te-d-une-acceleration-americaine_4618930_3234.html.

Lee-Makiyama, H. (2015) 'The Transatlantic Trade and Investment
Partnership: An Accident Report', January, www.ecipe.org/
publications/ttip-accident-report/?chapter=all.

Leonard, M. (2005) *Why Europe Will Run the 21st Century*.
London: HarperCollins.

Lester, S., and Barbee, I. (2014) 'Tackling regulatory trade barri-
ers in the Transatlantic Trade and Investment Partnership', in
D. Cardoso, P. Methumbu, M. Venhaus and M. Verde Garrido
(eds), *The Transatlantic Colossus: Global Contributions to
Broaden the Debate on the EU–US Free Trade Agreement*.
Berlin: Berlin Forum on Global Politics, pp. 84–8.

Lofsted, R. E. (2011) 'Risk versus hazard – how to regulate in
the 21st century', *European Journal of Risk Regulation*, 2(2):
149–68.

Macartney, H. (2014) *The Debt Crisis and European Democratic
Legitimacy*. Basingstoke: Palgrave Macmillan.

Malmström, C. (2014) 'Debating TTIP', speech delivered at the
Open Europe and Friedrich Naumann Stiftung, Brussels, 11
December, http://trade.ec.europa.eu/doclib/docs/2014/
december/tradoc_152942.pdf.

Malmström, C. (2015a) 'Three reasons why TTIP is good for
Austria', speech delivered in Vienna, 20 January, http://trade.

ec.europa.eu/doclib/docs/2015/january/tradoc_153054.
doc%20web.pdf.

Malmström, C. (2015b) 'TTIP: on course to deliver for the UK', speech delivered in London, 16 February, http://trade.ec.europa.eu/doclib/docs/2015/february/tradoc_153 142.pdf.

Malmström, C., and Hill, J. (2015) 'Don't believe the anti-TTIP hype – increasing trade is a no-brainer', *The Guardian*, 16 February, www.theguardian.com/commentisfree/2015/feb/16/ttip-transatlantic-trade-deal-businesses.

Manners, I. (2002) 'Normative power Europe: a contradiction in terms?', *Journal of Common Market Studies*, 40(2): 235–58.

Mauldin, W., and Hughes, S. (2014) 'Reid deals body blow to Obama on trade', *Wall Street Journal*, 29 January, www.wsj.com/articles/SB10001424052702303743604579350963039911616.

Meunier, S. (2005) *Trading Voices: The European Union in International Commercial Negotiations*. Princeton, NJ: Princeton University Press.

Meuwese, A. (2011) 'EU–US horizontal regulatory cooperation: mutual recognition of impact assessment?', in D. Vogel and J. F. M. Swinnen (eds), *Transatlantic Regulatory Cooperation: The Shifting Roles of the EU, the US and California*. Cheltenham: Edward Elgar, pp. 249–64.

Milevska, T. (2013) 'EU aviation emission proposals attacked from all sides', *EurActiv*, 15 November, www.euractiv.com/transport/commission-fails-comprehensive-p-news-531697.

Monbiot, G. (2013) 'This transatlantic trade deal is a full-frontal assault on democracy', *The Guardian*, 4 November, www.theguardian.com/commentisfree/2013/nov/04/us-trade-deal-full-frontal-assault-on-democracy.

Moody, G. (2014) 'TTIP update XXI: TTIP is worth an extra cup of coffee per person per week', *Computer World UK Blog*, 27 March, www.computerworlduk.com/blogs/open-enterprise/ttip-update-xxi-3569484/.

Moody, G. (2015) 'Why we should rename TAFTA/TTIP as the "Atlantic Car Trade Agreement"', *Techdirt*, 9 February, https://www.techdirt.com/articles/20150207/06040929944/why-we-should-rename-taftattip-as-atlantic-car-trade-agreement.shtml.

Morgan, B. (2003) 'The economisation of politics: meta-regulation as a form of nonjudicial legality', *Social Legal Studies*, 12(4): 489–523.

Morin, J. F. (2011) 'The life cycle of transnational issues: lessons from the access to medicines controversy', *Global Society*, 25(2): 227–47.

Myant, M., and O'Brien, R. (2015) *The TTIP's Impact: Bringing in the Missing Issue*, ETUI Working Paper 2015.01. Brussels: ETUI.

Narlikar, A. (2010) 'New powers in the club: the challenges of global trade governance', *International Affairs*, 86(3): 717–28.

Nicolaïdis, K., and Shaffer, G. (2005) 'Transnational mutual recognition regimes: governance without global government', *Law and Contemporary Problems*, 68(2): 263–317.

O'Connor Close, C., and Mancini, D. J. (2007) *Comparison of US and European Commission Guidelines on Regulatory Impact Assessment/Analysis*, Industrial Policy and Economic Reforms Papers no. 3. Brussels: European Commission.

Olson, M. (1965) *The Logic of Collective Action*. Cambridge, MA: Harvard University Press.

Peterson, J., Doherty, R., Van Cutsem, M., Wallace, H., Epstein, R., Burwell, F., Pollack, M. A., Quinlan, J. P., and Young, A. R. (2004) *Review of the Framework for Relations between the European Union and the United States. An Independent Study (Final Report)*. Brussels: European Commission.

Pew Research Centre (2014) *Support in Principle for U.S.-EU Trade Pact*. Washington, DC: Pew Research Centre; www.pewglobal.org/2014/04/09/support-in-principle-for-u-s-eu-trade-pact/.

Piermantini, R., and Teh, R. (2005) *Demystifying Modeling Methods for Trade Policy*, WTO Discussion Papers, no. 10. Geneva: WTO.

Polanyi, K. (1944) *The Great Transformation*. New York: Rinehart.

Pollack, M. A., and Shaffer, G. C. (2001) *Transatlantic Governance in the Global Economy*. Lanham, MD: Rowman & Littlefield.

Pollack, M. A., and Shaffer, G. C. (2009) *When Cooperation Fails: The International Law and Politics of Genetically Modified Foods*. Oxford: Oxford University Press.

Poulsen, L., and Berger, A. (2015) 'The Transatlantic Trade and Investment Partnership, Investor-State Dispute Settlement and China', *Columbia FDI Perspectives*, no. 140, 2 February, http://ccsi.columbia.edu/files/2015/02/No-140-Berger-and-Skovgaard-Poulsen-FINAL.pdf.

Poulsen, L., Bonnitcha, J., and Yackee, J. W. (2013) *Costs and Benefits of an EU–USA Investment Protection Treaty*, report prepared for the Department of Business, Innovation and Skills, April. London: LSE.

Poulsen, L., Bonnitcha, J. and Yackee, J. W. (2015) *Transatlantic Investment Protection*, CEPS Special Report no. 102, March. Washington, DC and Brussels: Center for Transatlantic Relations, Johns Hopkins University and Centre for European Policy Studies.

Prestowitz, C. (2015) 'The Trans-Pacific Partnership won't deliver jobs or curb China's power', *Los Angeles Times*, 22 January, www.latimes.com/opinion/op-ed/la-oe-prestowitz tpp-trade-pact-20150123-story.html.

Public Citizen (2013) *The Perils of the OIRA Review: Reforms Need to Address Rampant Delays and Secrecy*, June, www.citizen.org/documents/oira-delays-regulatory-reform-report.pdf

Public Citizen (2015) 'The Transatlantic "Free Trade" Agreement (TAFTA)', www.citizen.org/Page.aspx?pid=6037.

Puig, S. (2013) 'Emergence and dynamism in international organizations: ICSID, investor-state arbitration and international investment law', *Georgetown Journal of International Law*, 44(2): 531–607.

Rachman, G. (2012) 'Think again: American decline', in J. M.

McCormick (ed.), *The Domestic Sources of American Foreign Policy: Insights and Evidence*. Lanham, MD: Rowman & Littlefield, pp. 47–54.

Rasmussen, A. F. (2013) 'A new era for EU–US trade', speech delivered at the Confederation of Danish Industry, Copenhagen, 7 October, www.nato.int/cps/en/natolive/opinions_103863.htm.

Raza, W. (2014) 'Öffentliche Dienstleistungen in internationalen Handelsabkommen: Erfahrungen aus der GATS-2000 Debatte', in O. Prausmüller and A. Wagner (eds), *Reclaim Public Services: Bilanz und Alternativen zur Neoliberalen Privatisierungspolitik*. Hamburg: VSA, pp. 65–88.

Raza, W., Grumiller, J., Taylor, L., Tröster, B., and von Arnim, R. (2014) 'Assess TTIP: assessing the claimed benefits of the Transatlantic Trade and Investment Partnership', Austrian Foundation for Development Research; www.oefse.at/fileadmin/content/Downloads/Publikationen/Policynote/PN10_ASSESS_TTIP.pdf.

Reich, R. (2015) '"We're facing a vicious cycle": Robert Reich unloads on inequality, TPP & the real economic story', *Salon*, 17 February, www.salon.com/2015/02/17/were_facing_a_vicious_cycle_robert_reich_unloads_on_inequality_tpp_the_real_economic_story/.

Rodrik, D. (2011) *The Globalization Paradox: Democracy and the Future of the World Economy*. New York: W.W. Norton.

Rollo, J., Holmes, P., Parra, M. M., and Ollerenshaw, S. (2013) 'Potential effects of the EU–US economic integration on selected developing countries', *GREAT Insights*, 2(8): 14–16.

Ruggie, J. G. (1982) 'International regimes, transactions and change: embedded liberalism in the post-war order', *International Organization*, 36(3): 379–415.

S2B (2010) *EU Investment Agreements in the Lisbon Treaty Era: A Reader*. Amsterdam: Transnational Institute.

S2B (2013) *A Brave New Transatlantic Partnership: The Proposed EU-US Transatlantic Trade and Investment Partnership (TTIP/*

TAFTA) and its Socio-Economic & Environmental Consequences, www.tni.org/sites/www.tni.org/files/download/brave_new_ atlantic_partnership.pdf.

S2B (2015) 'Member groups', www.s2bnetwork.org/about-us/ member-groups/.

Scharpf, F. (1999) *Governing in Europe.* Oxford: Oxford University Press.

Schattschneider, E. E. (1935) *Politics, Pressure and the Tariff.* New York: Prentice Hall.

Schmidt, S. K. (2007) 'Mutual recognition as a new mode of governance', *Journal of European Public Policy,* 14(5): 667–81.

Scholte, J.-A. (2001) *Civil Society and Democracy in Global Governance,* Centre for Study of Globalisation and Regionalisation Working Paper no. 65/01. Coventry: CSGR.

Scholte, J.-A. (2003) 'The WTO and civil society', in B. Hocking and S. McGuire (eds), *Trade Politics: International, Domestic and Regional Perspectives.* 2nd edn, London: Routledge, pp. 146–61.

Scrieciu, S. S. (2007) 'The inherent dangers of using computable general equilibrium models as a single integrated modelling framework for sustainability impact assessment: a critical note on Böhringer and Löschel (2006)', *Ecological Economics,* 60(4): 678–84.

Sell, S. K., and Prakash, A. (2004) 'Using Ideas strategically: the contest between business and NGO networks in intellectual property rights', *International Studies Quarterly,* 48(1): 143–75.

Shapiro, M. (2007) *Exposed: The Toxic Chemistry of Everyday Products and What's at Stake for American Power.* White River Junction, VT: Chelsea Green.

Sheikh, S. (2015) 'TTIP diary: an early start aboard the NoTTIP Express', *Morning Star,* 5 February, https://www. morningstaronline.co.uk/a-ecc9-TTIP-Diary-An-early-start-aboard-NoTTIP-Express.

Siles-Brügge, G. (2014) *Constructing European Union Trade Policy: A Global Idea of Europe*. Basingstoke: Palgrave Macmillan.

Smith, E., Azoulay, D., and Tuncak, B. (2015) *Lowest Common Denominator: How the Proposed EU–US Trade Deal Threatens to Lower Standards of Protection from Toxic Pesticides*. Mountain View, CA: Center for International Environmental Law; http://ciel.org/Publications/LCD_TTIP_Jan2015.pdf.

Snow, D. A., and Benford, R. D. (1988) 'Ideology, frame resonance and participant mobilization', *International Social Movement Research*, 1(1): 197–217.

Socialists and Democrats Group (2015a) 'S&D Position Paper on Investor-State Dispute Settlement Mechanisms in Ongoing Trade Negotiations', 4 March, www.bernd-lange.de/imperia/md/content/bezirkhannover/berndlange/2015/sd_position_paper_on_isds_march_4_2015.pdf.

Socialists and Democrats Group (2015b) 'Out of the Crisis – A New Economic Model for Europe', www.socialistsanddemocrats.eu/policies/out-crisis-better-economic-model-europe.

Der Spiegel (2014) 'Mittelstandsumfrage: Firmen Setzen Wenig Hoffnung in Freihandelsabkommen', 14 May, www.spiegel.de/wirtschaft/unternehmen/ttip-mittelstand-setzt-kaum-hoffnung-in-freihandelsabkommen-a-968383.html.

Der Spiegel (2015) 'TTIP-Protesttag in Deutschland: Kostümiert gegen den Kapitalismus', 18 April, www.spiegel.de/politik/deutschland/ttip-deutsche-protestieren-gegen-freihandelsabkommen-a-1029358.html.

Stanford, J. (2003) 'Economic models and economic reality: North American free trade and the predictions of economists', *International Journal of Political Economy*, 33(3): 28–49.

Steffenson, R. (2005) *Managing EU–US Relations: Actors, Institutions and the New Transatlantic Agenda*. Manchester: Manchester University Press.

Steinzor, R. (2012) 'The case for abolishing centralized White House regulatory review', *Michigan Journal of Environmental and Administrative Law*, 1(1): 209–86.

Stiglitz, J. (2014) 'On the wrong side of globalization', *New York Times*, 15 March, http://opinionator.blogs.nytimes.com/2014/03/15/on-the-wrong-side-of-globalization/?_php=true &_type=blogs&ref=josephestiglitz&_r=1.

Stop TTIP (2015a) 'About the ECI campaign', https://stop-ttip.org/about-the-eci-campaign/.

Stop TTIP (2015b) 'Home – stop TTIP', https://stop-ttip.org/.

Strange, M. (2011) 'Why network across national borders? TANs, their discursivity, and the case of the anti-GATS campaign', *Journal of Civil Society*, 7(1): 63–79.

Strange, S. (1985) 'Protectionism and world politics', *International Organization*, 39(2): 233–59.

TACD (2013) 'Resolution on regulatory coherence in the Transatlantic Trade and Investment Partnership', DOC NO: 16/13, December. London: TACD.

Taleb, N. (2007) *The Black Swan: The Impact of the Highly Improbable*. New York: Random House.

Trachtman, J. P. (2007) 'Embedding mutual recognition at the WTO', *Journal of European Public Policy*, 14(5): 780–99.

Traynor, I., and Neslen, A. (2014) 'Bonfire of red tape proposed in "bid to keep Britain in EU"', *The Guardian*, 12 October, www.theguardian.com/world/2014/oct/12/eu-business-deregulation-concern-worker-rights.

UEAPME (2014) 'Speaking notes for Luc Hendrickx – INTE hearing: evaluating the Commission's term with regard to trade policy', 12 February, www.europarl.europa.eu/document/activities/cont/201402/20140224ATT79886/20140224ATT79886EN.pdf.

US Senate (2013) 'Baucus, Hatch outline priorities for potential U.S.–EU trade agreement', 12 February, www.finance.senate.gov/newsroom/chairman/release/?id=17b2fd73-067d-4a4a-a50f-a00265efbf67.

van Ham, P. (2013) 'The geopolitics of TTIP', Clingendael Policy Brief, no. 23. The Hague: Clingendael.

Van Harten, G. (2005) 'Private authority and transnational governance: the contours of the international system of investor protection', *Review of International Political Economy*, 12(4): 600–23.

Van Harten, G. (2014) *Comments on the European Commission's Approach to Investor-State Arbitration in TTIP and CETA*, Legal Studies Research Paper no. 59, http://papers.ssrn.com/sol3/papers.cfm?abstract_id=2466688.

Verhofstadt, G. (2006) *The United States of Europe*. London: Federal Trust.

Vincenti, D. (2014) 'US ambassador: beyond growth, TTIP must happen for geostrategic reasons', *EurActiv*, 16 July, www.euractiv.com/sections/trade-industry/us-ambassador-eu-anthony-l-gardner-beyond-growth-ttip-must-happen.

Vincenti, D. (2015) 'Brussels considers replacing ISDS with a public court', *EurActiv*, 19 March, www.euractiv.com/sections/trade-society/eu-considers-replacing-isds-public-court-313079.

Vogel, D. (1995) *Trading Up: Consumer and Environmental Regulation in a Global Economy*. Cambridge, MA: Harvard University Press.

Vogel, D. (2012) *The Politics of Precaution: Regulating Health, Safety and Environmental Risks in Europe and the United States*. Princeton, NJ: Princeton University Press.

Wade, R. H. (2003) 'What strategies are viable for developing countries today? The World Trade Organization and the shrinking of "development space"', *Review of International Political Economy*, 10(4): 621–44.

Wallach, L. (2012) 'Can a "Dracula strategy" bring Trans-Pacific Partnership into the sunlight?', *Yes Magazine*, 21 November, www.yesmagazine.org/new-economy/can-dracula-strategy-bring-trans-pacific-partnership-into-sunlight.

Wallach, L. (2013) 'The corporate invasion', *Le Monde Diplomatique*, 2 December, http://mondediplo.com/2013/12/02tafta.

Walter, A. (2001) 'NGOs, business, and international investment: the Multilateral Agreement on Investment, Seattle, and beyond', *Global Governance*, 7(1): 51–73.

Warkentin, C., and Mingst, K. (2000) 'International institutions, the state, and global civil society in the age of the world wide web', *Global Governance*, 6(2): 237–57.

Warren, E. (2015) 'The Trans-Pacific Partnership clause everyone should oppose', *Washington Post*, 25 February, www. washingtonpost.com/opinions/kill-the-dispute-settlement-language-in-the-trans-pacific-partnership/2015/02/25/ec7705 a2-bd1e-11e4-b274-e5209a3bc9a9_story.html.

Watson, M. (2014) *Uneconomic Economics and the Crisis of the Model World*. Basingstoke: Palgrave Macmillan.

Weisman, J. (2015) 'Congressional panels approve fast track for trade deal, with conditions', *New York Times*, 23 April, www. nytimes.com/2015/04/24/business/international/congres sional-panels-approve-fast-track-for-trade-deal-with-condi tions.html?_r=0.

Wettach, S. (2014) 'TTIP Gegner legen EU-Kommission lahm', *Wirtschafts Woche*, 19 July, www.wiwo.de/politik/europa/ de-gucht-spricht-von-attacke-ttip-gegner-legen-eu-kommis sion-lahm/10221432.html.

White House (2013a) 'Remarks by the president in State of the Union address', 12 February, Washington, DC: White House.

White House (2013b) 'Remarks by President Obama, U.K. Prime Minister Cameron, European Commission President Barroso, and European Council President Van Rompuy on the Transatlantic Trade and Investment Partnership', 17 June, Washington, DC: White House.

White House (2014) 'Remarks by the president in State of the Union address', 28 January, Washington, DC: White House.

White House (2015) 'Remarks by the president in State of the Union address', 20 January, Washington, DC: White House.

Whitehouse, S., Defazio, P., Boxer, B., Eshoo, A. G., Warren, E., Farr, S., Markey, E. J., Lee, B., Grijalva, R. M., Chu, J., and Lowenthal, A. (2014) 'Letter to Ambassador Froman', 9

July, www.whitehouse.senate.gov/news/release/members-of-congress-press-us-trade-rep-on-tar-sands-policy.

Wiener, B., Rogers, M. D., Hammitt, J. K., and Sand, P. H. (eds) (2010) *The Reality of Precaution: Comparing Risk Regulation in the United States and Europe*. London: RFF Press.

Wilkinson, R. (2014) *What's Wrong with the WTO and How to Fix It*. Cambridge: Polity.

Woll, C., and Artigas, A. (2007) 'When trade liberalization turns into regulatory reform: the impact on business–government relations in international trade politics', *Regulation & Governance*, 1(1): 121–38.

Woolcock, S. (2012) *European Union Economic Diplomacy: The Role of the EU in External Economic Relations*. Farnham: Ashgate.

Young, A. R. (2013) 'Regulators beyond Borders: The External Impact of the EU's Rules', paper presented at the 13th biennial EUSA conference, Baltimore, 9–11 May.

Zakaria, F. (2009) *The Post-American World and the Rise of the Rest*. London: Penguin.

Index

Page numbers in italics denote figures or tables